SHAKESPEARE'S LAND

SHAKESPEARE'S LAND

A Journey through
the Landscape of Elizabethan England

A.L. Rowse
John Hedgecoe

CHRONICLE BOOKS · SAN FRANCISCO

First Published in the United States 1987 by
Chronicle Books, San Francisco

Shakespeare's Land
A Mobius International Book

Library of Congress Cataloging in Publication Data

Rowse, A. L. (Alfred Leslie), 1903-
  Shakespeare's land.

  Includes index.
  1. Shakespeare, William, 1564-1616 — Homes and
haunts — Pictorial works. 2. Shakespeare, William, 1564-1616 —
Contemporary England — Pictorial works. 3. Literary land-
marks — England — Pictorial works. 4. England — Description
and travel — 1971-   — Views.
I. Hedgecoe, John.   II. Title.
PR2915.R68 1987   822.3'3 [B]   87-6576
ISBN 0-87701-462-0 (pbk.)

Distributed in Canada by
Raincoast Books
112 East 3rd Avenue
Vancouver, B.C. V5T 1C8
10 9 8 7 6 5 4 3 2 1

Chronicle Books
One Hallidie Plaza
San Francisco, CA 94102

Contents

Introduction

Shakespeare is the most autobiographical of all Elizabethan dramatists. If his soul is in his Sonnets his background and the world in which he lived permeate all he wrote.

There remains sufficient surviving evidence of the landscape and the times in which he moved for us to see much of what he saw. But we cannot know all the places he knew. We have little record of those visited by the Companies with which he was connected, particularly before the decisive year 1594, when the Lord Chamberlain's Company, of which he became a leading member, was founded. We do know that this Company visited Marlborough and Dover, while it was the favourite with both Elizabeth I and her successor James I, performing at court wherever it happened to be – at Whitehall, Windsor, Richmond, Greenwich – more frequently than any of the other Companies.

The first thing to strike a perceptive mind is that the author of both plays and poems was a countryman. This is in marked contrast to those urban, though not urbane, intellectuals Marlowe and Ben Jonson, both of whom he knew well, though he was a very different kind of man. William Shakespeare was a gentleman, courteous and smooth, tactful and prudent, never landing in trouble as they did. His university was that of nature: woodland and field and farm, upland pastures with their sheep-shearing feasts, the golden hills touched by the sun, rivers with their bridges and swans ('Sweet swan of Avon', Ben Jonson hailed him); country sports and pastimes: hare-coursing, hawking, archery, and, especially reflected in the early plays, hunting the deer.

Secondly, he was very familiar with London, and places around the Thames, a main highway in those days of unmetalled roads. We can trace him at Windsor, Eton, Datchet Mead; by Rochester, or along the routes from Stratford to London, one through Long Compton and Oxford, another along Watling Street by Southam, St Albans and the 'suburbs' of Holborn, into the City.

There is no likelihood that he ever went abroad in that hard-working, hard-pressed life, so early married and having to keep his little family at Stratford. John Aubrey tells us that, in those working years away from home, he went back to Stratford once a year, presumably in summer, for winter was busiest for the theatre in London and at Court.

Conjectures about Shakespeare, which have been legion, are utterly valueless – and superfluous – when we know more about him than about any other Elizabethan dramatist, and the facts are so revealing, the background so rich. We do not have to look out for him other than in the rough triangle of the South of England, from Stratford down the Avon Valley to the Severn; to Worcester, whither he went as a minor for special licence to get married right quick; thence southward to Thames-side, with the extension of Watling Street into Kent: to Rochester and Dover. We know that his Company played at Dover in August 1606, while that autumn he wrote *King Lear*, with its vivid description of the cliff that has become known as Shakespeare's Cliff.

Everywhere he went, that observant eye noticed the bare ruined choirs of the abbeys, the upturned brasses, the monuments. And, of course, people: again, the invaluable John Aubrey tells us that 'Ben Jonson and he did gather humours of men daily wherever they came . . . The humour of the constable' – evidently Dogberry in *Much Ado* – 'he happened to take at Grendon in Bucks, which is the road from London to Stratford'. Aubrey goes on to cite the familiar verses about one of the Combes at Stratford, neighbours along the street to the church, and with their monuments within the church. He ends up 'Vide his epitaph in Dugdale's Warwickshire'; and there we find, 'one thing more in reference to this ancient town is observable, that it gave birth and sepulture to our late famous poet, William Shakespeare'.

Warwickshire was already proud of its Stratford son who had made fame and fortune in the London theatre, who all his life retained contact with his native place, and retired there to die – an exchange of affection naturally corroborated by his will. 'In Warwickshire I have true-hearted friends . . .'.

*'a gentleman, courteous, tactful and prudent' . . . the best-known
likeness of William Shakespeare, the Chandos portrait in the National
Portrait Gallery, London.*

CHRONOLOGY

To English-speaking peoples, the age of the first Elizabeth and of Shakespeare is the most attractive period in the country's history. A start had been made on a 'united kingdom': Wales had been subdued and a Welsh family, the Tudors, ruled England; by the time of Shakespeare's death a Scotsman, James Stuart, was on the throne, the ground prepared for this marriage of nations by Elizabeth's grandfather, Henry VII, who married his daughter to the Scottish king, James IV.

─────────1500─────────

Henry VII, first Tudor monarch of England (crowned after death of Richard III at Bosworth Field, 1485) died, 1509

Henry VIII (1509–1547)

Edward VI (1547–1553)

─────────1550─────────

Jane Grey, nine days' queen, 1553

Mary I (1553–1558)

ELIZABETH I *(1558–1603)*

Drake circumnavigates the world (1577–1580)

Raleigh sent first English colony to North America (Roanoke, N. Carolina) 1585–6

Defeat of Spanish Armada (1588)

John Shakespeare m Mary Arden (1556)

William Shakespeare born (1564) marries Anne Hathaway (1582) Goes to London (c 1587)

Chronology of Plays: 1590–1 Henry VI (parts 1, 2, 3), Titus Andronicus, The Comedy of Errors; 1592–3 The Two Gentlemen of Verona, The Taming of the Shrew, Richard III; 1593–4 Love's Labour's Lost, A Midsummer Night's Dream; 1594–5 Richard II, Romeo and Juliet; 1596 King John, The Merchant of Venice; 1597–8 Henry IV (parts 1, 2), As You Like It; 1599 Henry V, Much Ado About Nothing;

─────────1600─────────

1600 Julius Caesar; 1600–01 Hamlet, Twelfth Night; 1601–02 The Merry Wives of Windsor; 1602–03 Troilus and Cressida, All's Well That Ends Well; 1604 Measure for Measure, Othello; 1605–06 Macbeth, King Lear; 1607 Antony and Cleopatra; 1607–08 Coriolanus, Timon of Athens; 1608–09 Pericles; 1609–10 Cymbeline; 1610–11 The Winter's Tale; 1611–12 The Tempest; 1612–13 Henry VIII.

Death of Shakespeare (1616)

JAMES I *(1603–1625) Gunpowder Plot (1605)*

First permanent English settlement, North America (Jamestown, Virginia) 1607

Henry VII His accession to the throne of England in 1485 brought to an end the dynastic struggle between the Houses of Lancaster and York. A happy peace was ensured when Henry, a Lancastrian, married Elizabeth of York. As king, Henry curbed the power of England's noble families and amassed a large fortune in the process. His legacy to his son, Henry VIII, was a strong, centralized government.

Henry VIII   *Formidable and self-willed, his break with the Church of Rome began the English Reformation and made him head of both Church and State. His seizure of the wealth and lands of the great religious houses replenished his coffers but brought to ruin the medieval glories of monastic architecture.*

Elizabeth I   *Daughter of Henry VIII's second wife (Anne Boleyn), she gave her name to a brilliant and exciting period of English history. Hers was an age of splendid heroes — Drake, Raleigh, Hawkins, Grenville — and of victories, like that over the Spanish Armada (1588). It was an age, too, of literary giants — Sidney, Spenser, Jonson, Marlowe and above all William Shakespeare.*

James I Stuart   *On his accession in 1603, the crowns of England and Scotland became one. James I was one of the most learned of monarchs, an author and sponsor, among other things, of the Authorized Version of The Bible (1611).*

SHAKESPEARE'S FAMILY TREE

The family tree of William Shakespeare. The direct line died out with Shakespeare's grandchildren, the last of whom died without issue in 1670. There are, however, living descendants of Shakespeare's younger sister, Joan.

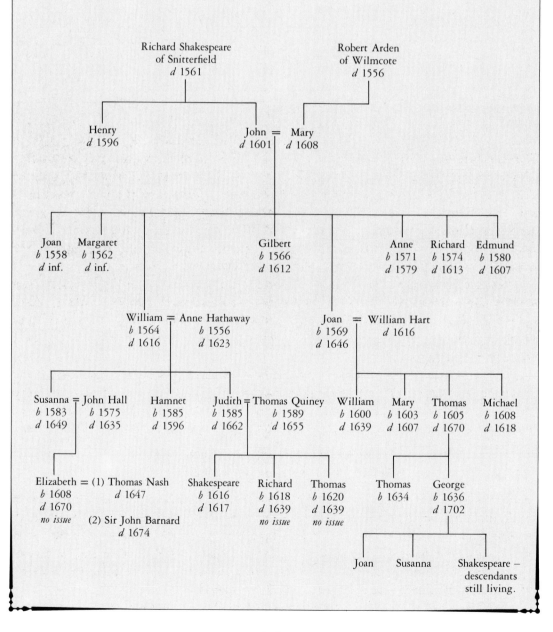

Stratford

The Shakespeares were very much Warwickshire folk. They came from the parish of Snitterfield, where William's father John and his uncle Henry were baptized in the font of the church. Snitterfield lies in the country a few miles north of Stratford, properly part of the ancient forest of Arden, a landscape characteristic of an older, wilder England. The River Avon separated this rough and wooded country from the southern part of Warwickshire known as the Feldon, with its richer, open fields and wide pastures looking up to the range of the Cotswolds on the horizon to south and west.

Shakespeare's mother was indeed of Arden, like the Shakespeares. Fortunately we have her family's house still with us, not far out of Stratford, at Wilmcote. When we come to *As You Like It* (1598), notable for several autobiographical touches and its references to the dead Marlowe, the book gives us Ardennes, but we need not doubt that the Forest of Arden is in mind.

In the earliest plays, the *Henry VI* trilogy, Warwickshire is given a good show – the prentice hand making the most of what he knows. Sir William Lucy, of neighbouring Charlecote, who was in fact sheriff of the county in that Henry's reign, is brought on in two or three scenes. A doughty fighter in France, he is given a tribute by Joan of Arc:

> *I think this upstart is old Talbot's ghost,*
> *He speaks with such a proud commanding spirit.*

Charlecote Park was begun only a few years before the infant William's baptism in Stratford church, on 26 April 1564. In the chapel at Charlecote we can see the effigies of the three knights, much as they looked in life, each of whom Shakespeare would have seen coming in or out of the town: Sir Thomas, who died in 1600, another Sir Thomas in 1605, a third in 1640. In the park there are still fallow deer – and we know the sporting countryman's fixation on hunting from all his early work.

In *Henry VI Part Three* the author makes a point of bringing the opposing forces to 'a plain in Warwickshire', 'a camp near Warwick', and of Edward IV's entry into the city of Coventry. Familiar places round about are all brought in: Dunsmore, the heath which the road skirts on the way; Daintry, the old and proper pronunciation of Daventry. Here enters Sir John Somerville, of a Warwickshire family connected with the Ardens; he has left Clarence 'at Southam with his forces'.

Another early play, *The Taming of the Shrew*, is given a specifically Stratford setting, for it is performed for the benefit of Christopher Sly, 'old Sly's son of Burton-heath'. This is Barton-on-the-Heath, where Shakespeare's uncle and aunt, the Lamberts, lived, not far from Moreton-in-Marsh. The country here could have been well described as 'ling, heath, broom, furze, anything'; under the lee of Brailes Hill, 'turfy mountains, where live nibbling sheep.' His mother's sister Joan married Edmund Lambert, and the names Joan and Edmund were carried on in the family in William's sister and youngest brother. A plot of land out there was inherited by Mary Arden and subsequently mortgaged to the Lamberts; the Shakespeares could never get it back. The medieval church they all knew still remains, with an Elizabethan brass of 1559 to Edmund Bury.

Christopher Sly owes a score (debt) for ale to Marian Hacket, 'the fat ale-wife of Wincot', a hamlet a few miles south of Stratford. Sly's crony, 'old John Naps of Greet', would be of a hamlet in the parish of Winchcombe, on the western edge of the Cotswolds. The First Folio misprinted Greece for Greet, which makes no sense; and editors with a superstitious veneration for the sacrosanctity of the printers' text have mostly preserved the misprint.

Stratford itself, the busy market town, hub of all this area, has remained providentially unspoiled – in spite of the ruin and degradation of the age we live in. I am sometimes asked in the United States whether it has not become 'commercialized'. Well, it grew and thrived by commerce, and today one must provide trinkets and mementoes for those who make the pilgrimage. The world should perhaps be glad that some guardian angel – or perhaps the sacred memory itself – has preserved it, as few historic places, from desecration.

William Shakespeare, if he returned to life, would have no difficulty in recognizing it all, from his birthplace at the top of Henley Street down to where the High Cross stood, where his father the Alderman had his standing as glover; along High street with some of its Elizabethan houses still there or re-fronted, past the unfortunate gap of New Place, across the way the Gild Chapel and Grammar School; then Church Street to the Old Town and the churchway to the welcoming porch of splendid Holy Trinity, where he and his family lie before the altar in the sanctuary.

In his time there was a smithy in Henley Street and below it a pair of cottages owned by a tailor. Hence in *King John*, which has a more touching recollection of his dead boy, Hamnet, we find:

> *I saw a smith stand with his hammer - thus,*
> *The whilst his iron did on the anvil cool,*
> *With open mouth swallowing a tailor's news,*
> *Who, with his shears and measure in his hand,*
> *Standing on slippers, which his nimble haste*
> *Had falsely thrust upon contrary feet.*

A familiar enough scene, but the detail of the slippers had not escaped those exceptionally observant eyes.

In the course of four centuries, there have had to be repairs and reconstructions, with some disappearances – most regrettably New Place itself, the fine five-gabled house which the theatre-man was able to buy when he began to prosper in London. (Anyhow, that had been rebuilt before it was pulled down in the 18th century by an irascible clergyman.) In Shakespeare's time a row of cottages ran down what is now Bridge street – an inn on either side, the Bear and the Swan – before coming to the Causey, and then Hugh Clopton's fine bridge, still functioning, if somewhat shakily.

The Birthplace was originally two cottages, one of them the glover's premises; though it needed to be propped up in the course of the centuries, I find it convincing within: the big original hearth downstairs, the principal chamber upstairs, as usual in Elizabethan houses. If one crosses over from the Birthplace to Rother (i.e. Cattle) Market, one comes to the White Swan, where there is a well-preserved wall painting of Tobit, his wife and son, with the Angel Raphael disguised – all in contemporary costume, gowns, hats, and breeches.

Thence one may walk down to Chapel Street and enter the Gild Chapel, where we see remains of the Doom (The Last Judgement) painted over the chancel arch – woodwork, rood-screen, images were taken down under the town's Protestant impulse. Stratford became Puritanical and Parliamentarian; Shakespeare's own family distinctly not. We can still hear the big bell that rung from the Chapel tower for his passing across the way; recast in 1591, it was repaired in 1615 in time for 'one sore sick that hears the passing-bell'.

The treasure chamber, with its vast chest for deeds and money, also contained the town's equipment of armour. We recall from *The Taming of the Shrew* that Petruchio was equipped with 'an old rusty sword ta'en out of the town armoury'. Next to it, across the courtyard, is the Grammar School, to which the more prosperous middle-class townsfolk sent their boys, the schoolrom intact. It was fairly regular in those days for a curate to teach younger children their ABC in the church porch.

So we come to the grand collegiate church of Holy Trinity, which was shorn of its college status at the Reformation, the chancel boarded off and left in disrepair. The College premises came to the prosperous Combes, with whom Shakespeare was friendly – they exchanged bequests in their wills. On the way through the churchyard was a charnel-house in his time; going up the churchway thither, I always think of the little page at the end of *Romeo and Juliet:*

> *I am almost afraid to stand alone*
> *Here in the churchyard; yet I will adventure.*

Juliet herself speaks:

> *Or nightly shut me in a charnel-house,*
> *O'er-covered quite with dead men's rattling bones.*

Or there is Puck, in *A Midsummer Night's Dream*, full of Stratford lore and characters:

> *Now it is the time of night*
> *That the graves, all gaping wide,*
> *Every one lets forth his sprite*
> *In the churchway paths to glide.*

In the great echoing church, draughty and unheated in those days, one cannot but hear:

> *When all aloud the wind doth blow,*
> *And coughing drowns the parson's saw.*

Then one looks down the long nave to the font where they were all baptized – broken by the beastly Puritans.

COVENTREE

THE ARMES
OF SUCH HONORA
BLE FAMYLIES AS
HAVE BENE EARLS
OF WARWICK

Henry of Nuburgh   John Marshall   John de Pleßeis

William Malduit   William Beauchamp   John Holland

Richard Nevill   George D. of Clarend   John Dudley

At Wolney in this Countye King Edward 4. gathering his forces to recover his former loßë,
was suddenly surprised and taken prisoner by his
brother George Duke of Clarence and Richard
the Stout Earle of Warwick and thence con-
veyed to the castell of Midleham in Yorkshire
whence shortly by escaped and came to London,
Anno Domini 1469.

Jodocus Hondius cælavit.

Around the church are monuments he knew. One, a tomb-chest between nave and the chapel of the Cloptons is that of the most important figure in Stratford history, Sir Hugh Clopton, who made his fortune as a mercer in London, of which he became Lord Mayor in 1492. He it was who built the chapel as a mausoleum for his family and – a great benefactor to the town – the bridge over the river. He was too the original builder of New Place, which Shakespeare was, rather grandly – so like him – to purchase and inhabit. Also in the chapel is the William Compton whom Shakespeare would have known, for he died in 1592.

The grandest tomb, an elaborate structure, is that of George Carew, Earl of Totnes, who married the Clopton heiress. A few years older than Shakespeare, he had an important career and a family base in Ireland, where he was Master of the Ordnance and President of Munster. Eventually he became Master-General of the Ordnance; a man of war, his tomb is encumbered by implements of war: guns, cannon, drums, flags.

He was also a bookish man, whose collections on Irish history garnish the Bodleian and Lambeth libraries. From about 1600 he was rebuilding the medieval house of the Cloptons, up on the slopes above the town; we still see his porch with Renaissance caryatids, and his panelled hall within. Shakespeare would at least have seen the great man on his comings and goings; the older man outlived him, so that he would not have seen the Caroline monument.

Other monuments he would have seen, and known the people: Richard Hill, for example, woollen draper, who had lived in Wood Street and died in 1593 (the year of *Venus and Adonis*, printed by the Stratford schoolfellow, Richard Field, in Blackfriars – to become so familiar). Then there is neighbour John Combe, with a monument from a Southwark workshop, where Shakespeare's was shortly to be made. Combe was well-to-do from money-lending, and an Elizabethan statute limited interest to 10 per cent. John Aubrey gives us an 'extemporary epitaph' his neighbour made on him:

> *Ten in the hundred the Devil allows,*
> *But Combe will have twelve, he swears and vows:*
> *If anyone asks who lies in this tomb,*
> *'Ho!', quoth the Devil, 'Tis my John a Combe,'*

No reason why these verses should not be the poet's, any more than the better known lines inscribed on his own gravestone. Shakespeare's bust looks down on the family gathered there: his wife Anne, some eight years older, who survived him by another seven years, dying in 1623, the year his collected plays were published – an exceptional tribute – by the Fellows of his Company. There too is his clever elder daughter, Susanna, who took after him as we learn from her epitaph: 'Witty above her sex' (the Elizabethan word 'wit' meant also intellect)...'Something of Shakespeare was in that'. So too her intelligent husband, Dr John Hall, who has left us his book of medical treatments of people around the county. It includes recipes for his daughter, Elizabeth, who ended Shakespeare's descendants as Lady Barnard, and also for Michael Drayton, Poet Laureate, friend of Shakespeare, and a regular summer visitor to the Rainsfords, across the meadows at Clifford Chambers. There, until it burned in this destructive century, stood their moated mansion and in the church their monument remains.

On previous page: *John Speed's map of Warwickshire: Speed,
historian and cartographer, was a contemporary of Shakespeare and,
like the poet, a provincial (from Cheshire) who made his name in
London. The map was one of a series called* The Theatre of the
Empire of Great Britain.

We return to the pivot of the town, the High Cross, which stood until Puritan ascendancy. 'I had as lief be whipped at the High Cross every morning', says a character in an early play. On our way out, on the right are the meadows where in Elizabethan days were the archery butts:

> *In my schooldays, when I had lost one shaft,*
> *I shot his fellow of the self-same flight*
> *The self-same way with more advisèd watch*
> *To find the other forth; and by adventuring both*
> *I oft found both.*

And so to Hugh Clopton's Bridge, southward to London.

Clopton Bridge, the 'fourteen arches of stone' spanning the Avon at Stratford (in Shakespeare's time almost wholly on the west bank of the river) was the only link between the town and the east and south of England. It was built in the fifteenth century, replacing an old hurdle causeway and, earlier, the ford which, in Saxon times, first gave the town its name – Straet-ford. It was built by Sir Hugh Clopton, the foremost citizen of Stratford in the fifteenth century, who became Lord Mayor of London.

[21]

Few traces now exist of the ancient forest which once clad Warwickshire north and west of the River Avon. Arden was Shakespeare's origin: his parents came from two of the scattered villages among the old woodlands, by that time being cleared – like similar forests throughout England – of its ancient cover, and being replaced by productive farmed land.

If the forest has all but vanished, its oakwood has survived the centuries best in the use it was put to by man, the half-timbered houses like those at Alcester, below, a Roman camp on the same road that gave Stratford its name, in which the Warwickshire countryside is still rich.

South and east of Clopton Bridge, the open landscape of 'Feldon' stretches east to the steep climb of Edgehill, fifteen miles to the east of Stratford, and south to the Cotswolds. It is prosperous farmland, since medieval times part of the great granary of central and eastern England – even in Shakespeare's time, a man-made landscape contrasting sharply with the wooded wilderness of Arden, beyond the Avon.

Violets, like cowslip, columbine and primroses, were hedgerow plants bedecking the countryside, and a poet's imagery.

*B*y its very nature, an important
ford across a river is a natural gathering place, drawing buyers and
sellers, craftsmen and labourers — and the ambitious, for whom it offers
talk of a wider world — from the surrounding countryside. William
Shakespeare's family provides a vivid example of this ancient process to
which countless towns and cities look for their origins.

The poet's grandfather, Richard Shakespeare, farmed land at
Snitterfield, a few miles north of Stratford, as tenant of Robert Arden,
of nearby Wilmcote. Of Richard's two sons, born at Snitterfield and
probably baptized there in the Church of St James, Henry stayed with
the farm; his brother John, the poet's father, took the road to Stratford,
set up as a glover and became a townsman.

*S*nitterfield
Church remains, largely unaltered in
appearance, above the meadows once farmed
by the Shakespeares, the bones of Richard
and Henry somewhere in its graveyard, the
font where Henry and John were baptized
still within.

*M*ary Arden's House at Wilmcote, the childhood home of
Shakespeare's mother, is a typical example of sixteenth-century country
building, its timbers set close together (wood was still plentiful – later
they were wider spaced and infilled with brick 'noggin'). The house is a
little grander than some hereabouts, as befitting the home of a minor
member of an old and distinguished Warwickshire family, the Ardens,
and proprietor of some land. The house had about eleven Arras
tapestries, showing that they were perhaps minor gentry.

*T*he house, three miles north-west of Stratford, is well preserved and
part of the itinerary of all pilgrims to the Shakespeare country.
Adjoining it there is an old columbarium with lodgings for more than
600 doves (for the table, not for ornament) and a countryside museum.

*S*mall *and unspoiled, the Church of St John the Baptist at Aston Cantlow – a mile or two from Wilmcote – advances its claim to the marriage of Shakespeare's parents on the grounds that the bride was a parishioner – and that no other parish lays claim to it. The church retains most of its medieval features, including the fifteenth-century font in which Mary Arden was probably baptized.*

*S hakespeare's birthplace in Henley
Street, Stratford, today stands free of adjoining buildings. In the poet's
time it was part of a continuous frontage, one small town house among
many, but — like its neighbours — built of identical materials to those of
his mother's birthplace: blue lias stone footings from the Wilmcote
quarries and a frame of green Arden oak.
When John Shakespeare brought Mary, his young wife, to his home and
thriving glover's business in Henley Street, the birthplace consisted of
two separate premises, one the family home, the other the glover's shop
and store. Subsequent generations set little store by literary shrines and
by the early nineteenth century the family home had become a butcher's
shop and the glover's premises an inn,* The Swan and Maidenhead.

Shakespeare's birthplace before its restoration. After visiting it in 1815, the American writer Washington Irving described it as 'a mean-looking edifice of wood and plaster.'

The birthplace garden is a modern creation: this view would not have been evident in the poet's time, when outbuildings and neighbouring premises would have jostled it.

The house was rescued from decay (The Times thought it might be carted to America and trundled about 'like a caravan of wild beasts') in 1847. Over the next 20 years the buildings on either side were removed to reduce the fire risk and careful restoration brought the house to a fair approximation of the family home in which the poet was born and grew to a young man.

Aptly described in the theatrical terminology of the nineteenth-century auctioneer, the sale of Shakespeare's birthplace is announced at the London Auction House, September 1847.

The interior of the birthplace at Stratford has been restored convincingly, its rooms furnished with Elizabethan and Jacobean furniture of the kind that a prosperous townsman's family would have had about them. There is an air of spaciousness that might have been less evident with the clutter of a young family around the house, but it allows its visitors (far more than any other house of its kind would have welcomed) a strong sense of the homely atmosphere the young Shakespeare would have felt. The kitchen, left, has a huge open hearth, furnished with contemporary utensils and, in the centre, a remarkable device to harness a child – helping it to learn to walk, but not into the fireplace.

The bedroom, above, in which William Shakespeare probably was born, is furnished in the manner of the time, with 'half-headed' bed, carved chest, and rocking cradle.

Close to, or from a distance, reflected in the waters of the Avon on its south side, the Collegiate Church of the Holy and Undivided Trinity, Stratford, is among the most beautiful of English parish churches. There was a monastery (of which nothing remains) at Stratford in Saxon times. The parish church itself dates from about 1200, with substantial additions to the fabric over the following three centuries.

The vista of the church today is much as Shakespeare would have known it, apart from the spire added many years after his death – and the graveyard headstones of later Stratford folk.

The record of his baptism (according to the custom of the old church, and in its language, Latin, as soon as possible after a child's birth) appears in the parish register –

April 26 Gulielmus filius
Johannes Shakspear

– and among its burial records of 1616, almost exactly 52 years later and now in English –

Aprill 25 Will Shakspear, gent.

As a leading citizen of the town, Shakespeare was buried in the chancel of the church, alongside his wife Anne, daughter Susanna, son-in-law John Nash, and Thomas Nash, the son-in-law of Hall.

High clerestory windows flood the knave of Holy Trinity with light, as they have for 500 years past, and in the aisles and transepts tombs and memorials recall people the poet would have known or who were part of the history of Stratford. Next to the Shakespeare family, the Cloptons are best-remembered, with their own chapel: the founder of their fortunes, Hugh Clopton, made his fortune in London, became its Lord Mayor and (as a man who made frequent journeys, and was aware of its importance) built Stratford's famous bridge, which bears his name.

More splendid even than the Clopton memorials – an eloquent example of Elizabethan art – is that of the Carews. George Carew, Earl of Totnes was sometime Master of Ordnance to James I, an office recalled in the carvings of guns, gunpowder barrels, and shot on the side of the memorial. The church remembers John Combe, a friend of Shakespeare (who left him a small legacy in his will) and Richard Hill, a worthy and much-admired magistrate whose tomb has inscriptions in four languages – Hebrew, Greek, Latin, and English.

Fifteenth-century misericords – hinged seats on which choristers took the weight off their feet during services – in the chancel of Holy Trinity.

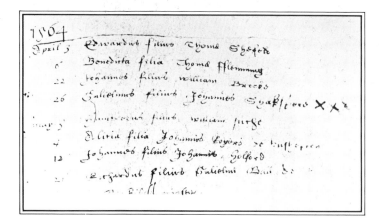

Shakespeare's birth entry in the parish register of Holy Trinity (now held in the safe keeping of the Birthplace Trust).

*A*fter the parish church of the Holy Trinity, the Gild Chapel and the
Gildhall adjoining it were the most important buildings in
Shakespeare's Stratford. The Gild of the Holy Cross had flourished in
the centuries before Shakespeare's birth, effectively providing the town
with its local government until it was suppressed during the
Reformation. In the form in which it now exists, the Chapel was the
benefaction of Hugh Clopton. Opposite it, he built New Place as his
home and here, now rich enough to purchase what was one of Stratford's
largest houses, Shakespeare came to end his days. An ornamental
garden now marks the site of New Place which was pulled down by a
later owner, an irascible clergyman, in 1759, after a quarrel with the
town authorities.

Shakespeare's schoolroom: in the 'over hall' above the armoury in the Gild House, Stratford Grammar School was already of some repute when the boy attended it, along with other burgesses' sons, in the 1570s. The half-timbered, fifteenth-century building was of modest size compared with some: Winchester, one of the earliest grammar schools, was as grand as a university college. The 'over hall' first became a schoolroom when the once-powerful Gild of the Holy Cross, whose chapel it adjoins, was dissolved during the reign of Henry VIII.

Lily's Latin Grammar, a schoolbook with which the young Shakespeare would have been familiar. It was the grammar book used in all Elizabethan Grammar Schools.

At the feet of the master – and in the shadow of the birch: a Tudor classroom. The illustration is a woodcut from Parvulorum Institutio, printed by Wynkyn de Worde.

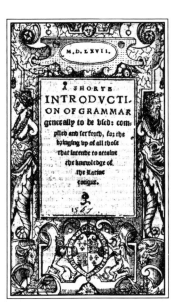

*A mile or so from his home at
Stratford, young William Shakespeare courted his wife-to-be, Anne
Hathaway, whose home was in the village of Shottery. 'Cottage' is
something of a misnomer for her birthplace, a farmhouse known as
Hewlands, on the fringe of Arden Forest. The Hathaways were
comfortably off, farming scores of acres in the neighbourhood, as they
had done for generations and were to continue to do, long after: there
were Hathaways at Hewlands until the 1890s.*

Impeccably maintained by the Birthplace Trust, Anne Hathaway's Cottage is perhaps the most popular of houses associated with the poet, set in a garden of flowers, herbs, and plants typical of the poet's time and referred to in his plays.

*T*he interior of Anne Hathaway's Cottage is
scrupulously maintained in the way it would have
been in Shakespeare's day. The principal bedroom at
the top of the stairs includes the original joists and
timberwork. Among the fine oak furniture in the
Cottage is the famous Hathaway bedstead.
Splendidly carved and dating from the late 16th
century, it remained the property of the Hathaway
family until 1892, when it was bought by the
Birthplace Trust.

*A*s *Shakespeare's son-in-law and*
a well-known doctor throughout Warwickshire, John Hall would have
attended the poet during his last illness. Hall married Susanna
Shakespeare in 1607 and bought Hall's Croft, where Shakespeare's
grandchild, Elizabeth, was born a year later. Part of the house was set
aside for the doctor's practice and one room is now furnished in the style
of an Elizabethan dispensary.

**Select Observations
ON
ENGLISH
BODIES:**
OR,
Cures both Empericall and
Historicall, performed up-
on very eminent Per-
sons in desperate
Diseases.

First, written in Latine
by Mr. *John Hall* Physician,
living at *Stratford* upon *Avon*
in *Warwick-shire,* where he
was very famous, as also in
the Co nties adjacent, as ap-
peares by these Observations
drawn out of severall hundreds of his, as choysest.

Now put into English for com-
mon benefit by *James Cooke*
Practitioner in *Physick* and
Chirurgery.

London, Printed for *John Sherley,* at the
Golden Pelican, in *Little-Britain.* **1657.**

John Hall enjoyed a high reputation during his lifetime, travelling the county to attend leading families. Among his patients was Shakespeare's friend, the poet Michael Drayton, whose complaint – and its cure – are found in one of the doctor's casebooks:

Mr Drayton, an excellent poet, labouring of a tertian {*ague*}, was cured by the following: the emetic infusion one ounce, syrup of violets a spoonful, mix them . . .

Extracts from John Hall's casebooks were published 20 years after his death. These Select Observations on English Bodies *offer a good illustration of Elizabethan medical practice.*

With its predecessor, the Gild Chapel, visible in the distance, Stratford's Town Hall did not exist in Shakespeare's time – it is eighteenth-century Palladian – but from a niche in its north wall, the statue of the poet looks down on a street he knew well. The statue was given to the town by David Garrick, the most celebrated actor of his time, in 1769, when he organized a three-day festival in honour of the poet. The festival was washed out by rain.

The apocryphal figures of Tobit, his wife and son disguised in Elizabethan costume, in a well-preserved wall painting at the White Swan, Stratford.

The Old Bank, formerly the Old Market Hall, in the High Street, like many of Stratford's buildings, emphasizes the town's association with Shakespeare.

*Harvard House: Shakespeare
would have known this house well, but not by its modern name. When
he was a child, it was called 'The Ancient House' a wattle-and-daub
structure that had stood on the site for more than 300 years. He was at
the height of his fame in London when fire devastated much of Stratford
— a commonplace event in those days of tinder-box houses of wood and
thatch — and The Ancient House was among those damaged. What was
left was bought by a master butcher, Thomas Rogers, who rebuilt and
enlarged it, with its handsomely carved exterior one of the most striking
buildings of Elizabethan Stratford.
Rogers had 13 children, one of whom, Katherine, married Robert
Harvard of Southwark in London. Their son John emigrated to
America, and although he died when he was only 30, left a will which
led to the founding of Harvard College, subsequently University. The
house was bought by an American businessman in 1909 and presented
in trust to the University.*

*Now furnished in the manner of
Shakespeare's day, The Ancient House was alive with people when
Thomas Rogers rebuilt it — his own family of 15 with a half-dozen
live-in servants, butcher's apprentices, and maids-of-all-work living
above the ground floor which was the shop, slaughterhouse, and store.*

Warwickshire and the Cotswolds

Beyond Clopton Bridge, the Feldon highways head toward the Lucy mansion at Charlecote, to Banbury, and south to Shipston-on-Stour, Oxford, and London. At Alveston, now practically a suburb of Stratford, there is a reminder of a scandal attaching briefly to Shakespeare's family – to his eldest daughter, Susanna. There is a curious upright slab with a figure of Nicholas Lane, gent., who died in 1595, with tall ruff and dagger at side, his children grouped at his feet. A nephew, scapegrace John, grew up to be haled before the Consistory Court in Worcester Cathedral by Dr Hall for libelling Susanna, the latter's wife, saying that she had 'the running of the reins', i.e. a venereal infection. This slander was reported by a family friend, who became a witness to Shakespeare's will a couple of years later.

The country around here, the rising ground up to Bishopton and Welcombe, had a close connection with Shakespeare. He invested the larger part of his fortune in a moiety of the tithes hereabouts, and later we learn that he was 'not able to bear the enclosing of Welcome', where there was trouble over enclosures. His other large investment was in the purchase of 107 acres of the best land in Old Stratford, around the church. His son-in-law, Dr Hall, would have been able to keep his eye on the property from Hall's Croft just up the road.

Let us go along the road into the north of the county with Shakespeare, to Warwick, the county town, where his kinsmen the Greenes lived. The splendid mass of the Castle with its towers still dominates the historic town as it did in his time, rising up on its cliff above the Avon, comparable to Windsor. Up to 1590 the Castle was in the possession of Ambrose Dudley, Earl of Warwick. Then James I granted it to the poet-dramatist Fulke Greville, Lord Brooke, in whose family it thenceforward remained, with all its historic and artistic treasures, until our own time, when it has been 'saved' for tourists.

Nevertheless, Warwick retains many things Shakespeare would have known. In the church, the Beauchamp Chapel has one of the most splendid medieval monuments with its touching bronze effigy, enamels, brass plate and copper gilt – a grand work of art. This

Beauchamp Earl of Warwick appears briefly in *Henry V.* Also here lies the princely Leicester, with his second wife, Lettice Knollys, and their little boy Robert, 'the Noble Impe', who has a plaque to himself. A page to the Queen, he was nine when he died; his little suit of chain-armour used to be shown in the hall of the Castle. Leicester's elder brother, Ambrose, also has his tomb here, along with his widow, who was the queen's chief intimate in her last years. Over the West Gate of the town is the delightful group of Leycester's Hospital, the almshouses he founded in recognition of his good fortune, with the chapel over the gate. Far from a Puritan himself, he was their patron and appointed the horrid Cartwright as its Master.

Further along the road is the magnificent mass of ruined Kenilworth. Pevsner waxes poetic about it:

> . . .*of the ruinous castles of England Kenilworth is one of the grandest. It has superb Norman, 14th century, and Elizabethan work; and where, as on the way back from the Pleasaunce, one sees all three together and all three in the strong yet mellow red of their sandstone, the view could not be bettered.*

In Elizabeth I's time it was still more striking, for the rose-red walls and towers were reflected in a great lake that extended round the south side. Here were held the water-pageants of the famous Kenilworth Entertainments for the Queen in 1575, to which all the country flocked from roundabout. William Shakespeare was then a boy of eleven, old enough to register the scene on the lake:

> *Thou rememberest*
> *Since once I sat upon a promontory,*
> *And heard a mermaid on a dolphin's back . . .*

And:

> *a fair Vestal, thronèd by the west.*
> *But I might see young Cupid's fiery shaft*
> *Quenched in the chaste beams of the watery moon;*
> *And the imperial Votaress passed on,*
> *In maiden meditation, fancy-free.*

The splendid shows were laid on as Leicester's last effort to capture the maiden hand of the Vestal virgin: Warwickshire would have known the gossip.

Some seven miles north-west of Warwick is the beautiful moated Elizabethan house of Baddesley Clinton, providentially preserved: gateway, tall decorative chimneys; and, within, the panelled hall, ornate chimney-pieces, and heraldic glass. All is mostly the handiwork of admirable Henry Ferrers, the antiquarian. What fun he must have had in doing it! His life spanned Shakespeare's at both ends: 1549–1633. Camden pays tribute to him: 'a man both for knowledge of antiquity very commendable and my especial friend'. The family remained there in that blissful house, in direct line, from medieval times to the late Victorian age.

Coventry was the cathedral city of North Warwickshire. We know that Lord Strange's men, with whom Shakespeare had some connection before the formation of the Lord Chamberlain's Company gave him security, paid it a visit in 1587–8. The medieval

The River Avon at Charlecote, with the lovely, pinnacled church at Hampton Lucy visible across the water meadows.

monastic cathedral was laid low by the Reformation, leaving the two splendid churches of Holy Trinity (gutted by German bombs in our time) and St Michael's. Ben Jonson's headmaster, William Camden, describes it as it was: 'a city very commodiously seated, large, sweet and neat, fortified with strong walls and set out with right goodly houses; amongst which there rise up on high two churches of rare workmanship, standing hard by the other and matched as it were concurrents'.

The city was eviscerated in the air raids of 1940, giving rise to a typical, if temporary, term in the German language, *Coventriert* ('Coventrated'). Yet, in and out the modern mess, there are still remains of an earlier age: the collegiate church of St John, the fine medieval steeple of Greyfriars; Tudor, timber-framed Ford's Hospital, the 14th century chapel of St John's Hospital. St Mary's Hall is the original Gildhall, with its eloquent complex of panelled parlours, roofs with heraldic bosses, stained glass, and statues from the original Market Cross (destroyed by Puritan barbarians earlier). There is also a resplendent tapestry of Henry VII's time, representing the Assumption of the Virgin. Everything speaks – or rather spoke – of the civic pride of the place as it once was. Falstaff reflects it for us, when he speaks of the rag-tag-and-bobtail he has picked up by way of recruits: 'I'll not march with them through Coventry, that's flat'. Further afield we have Sutton Coldfield, beyond Birmingham, and now practically a suburb of it: 'We'll to Sutton Co'fil' tonight', he says, evidently using the old pronunciation. The Tudor Bishop Veysey was a native, a benefactor of the town and church, of which he built north and south chapels, in one of which rests his tomb with painted effigy.

Returning to Stratford from the Arden country of North Warwickshire, we turn west to Shottery past Anne Hathaway's cottage – in her day Hewlands Farm – and up the hill to Alcester, of early Roman settlement, as the name shows. A curve in an old street shows a nice group of timber-framed houses, and at the back of the partly-rebuilt church of St Nicholas stands the tomb of Fulke Greville's parents, of 1559. A mile or two up the road is Coughton Court of the Throckmortons (still there!) with its palatial gatehouse and inner court, where the fearful ladies of that Catholic household waited for news of the Gunpowder Plot of 1605, in which their silly menfolk were involved. In the old church are the tombs and brasses of this faithful family, who went on being buried in their ancestral, if Anglican, church though remaining undeviating Catholics.

No time to cut up across country to Bearley, where Shakespeare's aunt Margaret lived, nor on to Henley-in-Arden, where he would have known the church, the old Gildhall next to it, and the tall shaft (only) of the market-cross in the long High Street – I suppose for the sheep-fairs, like St Giles's at Oxford. We must stick to the main road west to Worcester; the southern route by Bidford bridge over the Avon, with its original medieval cut-waters, is somewhat longer. We know that at the end of November 1583, as a bright spark of rising nineteen, he rode to Worcester with two Shottery friends as sureties to get his licence to marry from the bishop's registry (the southern part of Warwickshire was in that diocese). He knew 'swift Severn's flood' all right – notoriously more swift than Thames or Avon; the 'sandy-bottomed' Severn, and its 'sedgy banks'.

From Stratford one sees the Cotswolds on the skyline south into Oxfordshire and running away south-west to their steep escarpment into Gloucestershire. To Elizabethans rough hill-tops were 'mountains':

> *Full many a glorious morning have I seen*
> *Flatter the mountain-tops with sovereign eye . . .*

The Cotswolds – heavenly countryside – held not only the grand woollen churches, grey manor-houses, and delicious towns like Chipping Campden, for which we value it today, but in those days sported hare-coursing (as in *Venus and Adonis*), greyhound racing, Morris dancing and the well-known Cotswold Games, founded by Captain Dover and described by Jacobean poets. And so: 'How does your fallow greyhound, sir? I heard say he was outrun on Cotsall', i.e. Cotswold. One of Justice Shallow's swinge-bucklers, when he was a young fellow at the Inns of Court, was 'Will Squeal, a Cotswold man'. Old Shallow is a Justice of the Peace in the county of Gloucester; hence the country talk in his garden with Falstaff, with the references to Wincot (Wilnecote); Barson (Barcheston), where the famous Sheldon tapestries were made; and Hinckley Fair, just over the Warwickshire border in Leicestershire. Further afield, 'How a good yoke of bullocks at Stamford Fair?' The fairs were the great marts of the year in those days.

Shallow's cousin Slender is called a 'Banbury cheese' – Banbury Cross, more familiar from the nursery rhyme, is not mentioned. Banbury is along one of the south-eastern routes to London, and in its neighbourhood survives medieval and moated Broughton Castle, even now in the possession of the Saye-and-Sele family, whose ancestor appears tragically in *Henry VI Part Two*. From Stratford Bridge, turn southward again, through Alderminster, which in Shakespeare's time was owned by an executor of his will, Sir Thomas Russell of Strensham by the Severn. On we go through Shipston-on-Stour, past the little church of Long Compton, up the steep hill out of the Vale of the Red Horse and across the Romans' Fosseway into Oxfordshire. On our right up there are the prehistoric Rollright Stones, with all their folklore about the King and his Men, just an arrow-shot off the road. Not far off is exquisite, unspoiled Chastleton, being built about this time by Walter Jones, the rich Witney wool-merchant, who filled his house with good things, including Sheldon tapestries now dispersed. And so, through Chipping Norton, and on to Oxford.

A mile or so east of Clopton Bridge, the small church at Alveston contains the effigy of Nicholas Lane, squire of the manor. The lives of the Lanes of Alveston touched on those of the Shakespeares in several ways. Nicholas lent money to the poet's Uncle Henry and sued Shakespeare's father for the debt. Another member of the family, John Lane, was sued by Shakespeare's daughter Susanna for defamation.

A friend of Shakespeare both in London and Stratford, the Warwickshire poet Drayton regularly visited his patrons, the Rainsfords at Clifford Chambers, across the fields from Stratford. In his poetry there is a section which describes his — and Shakespeare's — native Warwickshire:

That shire which we the heart
of England well may call . . .

Shakespeare was two years old when Queen Elizabeth visited Charlecote, the fine mansion in the Stratford neighbourhood, on her way from visiting Kenilworth and Warwick. It was the family home of the Lucys, one of whom earns a mention in the Henry VI trilogy as a fighter in the French wars, his valour remarked upon by Joan of Arc. An earlier Lucy had arrived to save the day when Harry Hotspur was beset by the Scots at the Battle of Neville's Cross.

*D*eer still roam Charlecote Park where, ancient tradition has it, young Shakespeare was an enthusiastic hunter. It was with such young men in mind that Sir Thomas Lucy, a Member of Parliament for Warwickshire, endeavoured to push an anti-poaching bill through Parliament in 1584. Shakespeare was an out-of-doors sporting man with a fixation for deer hunting that permeates his early plays – 'my sportive blood' – in contrast to his contemporaries, Jonson and Marlowe.

*E*lizabeth I picnics: visits to great houses gave the monarch and her entourage an opportunity to sample the pleasures of country life.

The tomb in Charlecote Church of Sir Thomas Lucy (d.1600) and his wife. The dowry his 13-year-old bride brought to her marriage enabled him to pull down his old house and build anew – a characteristic Elizabethan mansion .

This illustration from Turbeville's Booke of Hunting *(1573) shows Elizabeth I at the successful conclusion to a deer hunt.*

*T*oday the most romantic of ruins, Kenilworth
Castle was in its splendid heyday during
Shakespeare's lifetime. He would have known it
well, a morning's walk 12 miles north of his home
at Stratford. The 'Kenilworth Entertainments' of
1575 may well have been attended by the young
Shakespeare, since countryfolk flooded in to see them.

  Elizabeth I had granted Kenilworth a year before
Shakespeare's birth to her favourite, Robert Dudley,
Earl of Leicester. In its time, it had been owned by
King John and John of Gaunt. During the Civil
war, it became a natural target for the
Parliamentary forces, who brought it to ruin.

*T*he prospect of Kenilworth Castle from the south
side of the old park from Sir William Dugdale's
Antiquities of Warwickshire (1830).

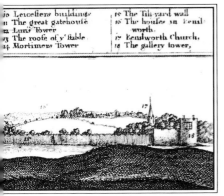

10 Leicesters buildings
11 The great gatehouse
12 Lunf Tower
13 The roofe of y' stable
14 Mortimer Tower

15 The Tilt yard wall
16 The houses in Kenil-
   worth.
17 Kenilworth Church.
18 The gallery tower,

One of the finest of all medieval fortress-homes, Warwick Castle stands on a rocky eminence above the River Avon, which protects its southern flanks. Most of the present building was erected after the thirteenth century, but defensive works of sorts had occupied the site, close to the boundaries of the Danelaw, since the days of Alfred the Great. Work on the building as it now is was begun by the Beauchamp family, the line founded by Henry de Newburgh, first Earl of Warwick.

The castle was granted by Queen Elizabeth to Ambrose Dudley (elder brother of Leicester) whom she made Earl of Warwick. James I subsequently granted it to Fulke Greville (descendant of the great woolstapler, Edward Grevel, of Chipping Camden).

Coats-of-arms of notable Warwickshire families – those of Beauchamp, Neville, and Dudley.

Robert Dudley, Elizabeth's favourite, lies in the richly decorated Beauchamp Chapel of St Mary's Church, Warwick. The chapel, built in the mid-fifteenth century, in the Perpendicular style, survived a ruinous fire that destroyed most of the church — as well as much of the town of Warwick — in 1694.

*L*ord Leycester's Hospital. Set above Warwick's West Gate, the fifteenth-century Hospital is still fulfilling the function it had in Elizabethan times, as almshouses for old soldiers. The building was originally owned by the medieval Gild of St George until the Gild was dissolved during the reign of Henry VIII. Here, Fulke Greville received James I.

*D*etail of timberwork of Lord Leycester's Hospital.

The Roman settlement from which Alcester takes its name covered the road west from Stratford at the point where it crosses the River Alne, a tributary of the Avon. Some half-timbered architecture survives here from Tudor times: and here, also, in the church of St Nicholas lies (with his wife) Fulke Greville, sometime Recorder of Stratford and well known to the Shakespeares and their neighbours. His better-known son, another Fulke Greville, the poet, was granted Warwick Castle – and was eventually murdered there by his manservant.

A long the Alne from Alcester, Henley-in-Arden flourished as a market in wool and wood.

The home of one family, the
Throckmortons, for more than 500 years, Coughton Court, a few miles
from Shakespeare's home, was mostly of recent construction in his
lifetime. The great gatehouse, built in 1509, houses a room in which
wives of the Gunpowder Plot conspirators heard news of their failure:
the Throckmortons were devout Catholics – and fecund, too. George
Throckmorton, who built the gatehouse, had eight sons and 11
daughters, and lived to see 112 grandchildren.

The Gunpowder Plotters: their
doomed attempt to restore Catholicism to England led them to a grisly
end – dragged through the streets of London to St Paul's Churchyard,
there to be hanged, drawn, and quartered.

*Th*e moated manor house of Baddesley Clinton is
another Warwickshire home associated with a
notable family: generations of Ferrers lie beneath the
floor of the parish church, one of them Henry
Ferrers, a contemporary of Shakespeare.

*H*enry Ferrers, antiquarian and scholar, was
responsible for altering and modernizing Baddesley
Clinton. He constructed the Great Hall in the
1580s and filled the house with ornate chimney
pieces, decorative panelling and heraldic glass of the
type seen here.

Worcester was perhaps the westernmost part of England to be visited by Shakespeare. His intended wife Anne Hathaway was pregnant and William, 18½ years old (Anne Hathaway was eight years older) was obliged to ride to Worcester to obtain a special licence to marry her – Stratford and South Warwickshire were part of the diocese of Worcester.

The bridge at Bidford-on-Avon, a village well-known to the poet. The medieval cutwaters of the bridge survive today, although it was damaged during the Civil War.

*T*he galleried courtyard of the New Inn, Gloucester, is typical of the
grander type of inn surviving from Shakespeare's day. In his time as a
member of a touring company of actors, inn yards, with their ever-
present nucleus of regulars and passing travellers, were the closest thing
to a theatre existing in the provinces.

*G*loucester Cathedral, with its fine Perpendicular work on the exterior
and central Norman tower, dominates the city. It is likely that
Shakespeare would have known both city and cathedral.

*A*t *Tewkesbury, the
Warwickshire Avon loses its identity in 'swift Severn's flood'. The town
and its abbey loomed large in the affairs of the kingdom less than a
century before Shakespeare's birth, when in 1471 the Yorkists routed
and slaughtered Lancastrians outside and within the abbey church.*

*England has no part more
endearing than the Cotswold Hills, where landscape, historic villages
and towns testify to the wealth of the medieval wool trade. Here was the
heart of English sheep farming: Cotswold wool was the best to be got in
England and English wool the best in Europe. Cotswold men and their
ways were close to Shakespeare and make their appearance in his plays:
The Winter's Tale produces an unforgettable portrayal of a sheep-
shearing feast.*

'Februarie' from The Shepheardes Calendar *by Immerito, a
pseudonym for Edmund Spenser (1579)*

*M*ulti-coloured bricks, from pink to darkest
umber, give Compton Wynyates perfection set in a
hollow of Edge Hill some miles south-east of
Stratford. A village was displaced to make way for
its parklands when it was built by Sir William
Compton in the early 1500s. Henry VIII, his
daughter Elizabeth I and her successors James I and
Charles I all stayed here.

*S*hakespeare often drew on the inspiration of the
familiar and well-loved Cotswolds for country
backgrounds and scenes.

*T*o the young Shakespeare, the Cotswold Hills became a familiar
playground and later provided inspiration for rural scenes in several
plays. Perhaps the best-known example is Justice Shallow's pleasant
house in the Cotswolds in Henry IV.

*G*reet, near Winchcombe, was
the home of old John Nats in The
Taming of the Shrew.

*M*ay-time was a traditional time for celebration in the agricultural
year and one associated particularly with young lovers.

*M*oated still, as a fortified manor
house, Broughton lies close to one of the main routes from Stratford to
London – that through Banbury. It was acquired by William of
Wykeham, Bishop of Winchester and founder of Winchester School and
New College, Oxford. It came into the hands of Sir William Fiennes,
Lord Saye and Sele in 1451, and the same family still lives there. The
whole house and its interior are remarkably unchanged, and
wonderfully evoke the atmosphere of past centuries.

Queen Anne's Room, Broughton Castle.

*B*arton-on-the-Heath, below.
Shakespeare's aunt, Joan Lambert, lived here, and his mother, Mary
Arden, owned a plot of land: his parents mortgaged the land to the
Lamberts, and could never get it back. Lawyer Robert Dover, founder
of the 'Cotswold Games' – horse racing, hare coursing, wrestling, and
dancing – a few years before Shakespeare died, is buried in the
churchyard.

*F*olklore surrounds the
weatherworn Rollright Stones, in Cotswold country between Barton-on-
the-Heath and Chipping Norton, along the road from Stratford to
Oxford. The King Stone, *the* King's Men *and the conspiratorial*
Whispering Knights *stand beside a prehistoric trackway bisecting*
England from the Humber to Salisbury Plain and beyond.

Grevel's House, Chipping Campden 'The flower of the wool merchants of England'. William Grevel built his house in Chipping Campden towards the end of the fourteenth century. The town was one of the most important of wool trading centres in the Cotswolds. Built, like most other houses hereabouts of the honey-coloured local stone, Grevel's House reflected its owner's position as one of the leading merchants to benefit from England's most important medieval export.

*A*stride the boundary between Gloucestershire and Oxfordshire, Chastleton House is a perfect expression of Elizabethan taste. It was built by a Witney wool merchant, Thomas Jones, in 1603. During the Civil War, one of his descendants, a Royalist, was chased home from the Battle of Worcester (1651). He was saved by his wife, who drugged his pursuers when she gave them food.

*C*hastleton once possessed examples of the famous Sheldon Tapestries, made on looms not far away at Barcheston Manor (Shakespeare's 'Barson'). The tapestries give a picture of Elizabethan topography and country life. Others portray coats-of-arms on cushions and the like.

Oxford

Shakespeare knew Oxford well enough. In 1592 the Queen paid the university a state visit, accompanied by Southampton among other grandees. So, in a play in the next twelve or eighteen months, we find the scene:

> *Where I have come great clerks have purposèd*
> *To greet me with premeditated welcomes;*
> *Where I have seen them shiver and look pale,*
> *Make periods in the midst of sentences,*
> *Throttle their practised accent in their fears,*
> *And in conclusion dumbly have broke off.*

Just such a break-down occurred in a timid don's speech of welcome. Southampton was a Cambridge man, but was incorporated Master of Arts on this occasion. The poet may well have been in attendance on his young patron; though not a university man, he knew the proper academic term for becoming an M.A.:

> *Proceeded well, to stop all good proceeding.*

Some folklore about his Oxford acquaintance goes right back to Aubrey in the next generation — and there is usually something in what he has to tell us. The vintner who kept the Crown tavern, John Davenant, had an intelligent and beautiful wife, 'of conversation extremely agreeable'. On his journeys to and from Stratford 'Master William Shakespeare did commonly lie at this house in Oxon, where he was exceedingly respected'. Aubrey scored out that he had heard 'Parson Robert Davenant say that Master W. Shakespeare has given him an hundred kisses'. However, another of Mistress Davenant's boys, the Cavalier dramatist, Sir William, liked to say over a glass of wine with his intimates that 'he writ with the very spirit that Shakespeare and seemed contented enough to be thought his son'. Then (again scored out): 'he would tell them the story as above, in which way his mother had a very light report'. What is certain is that the two Williams had a good deal in common: poetry and drama, both were sexy and keen on women, and, not least, their imaginative daring and genius.

Naturally a good deal of the Oxford that Shakespeare would have known remains. Coming into the city from Woodstock he would pass St Giles's Church, then the front of St John's College, where James I was received with a performance of Three Sybils – which may or may not have been caught up into *Macbeth*, which certainly was written to honour the Scottish King. Carfax is the centre, with the tower of the city church of St Martin's looking across to where the Golden Cross still has its old innyard. Further along Cornmarket is the Anglo-Saxon tower of St Michael at the North Gate, and an ancient house, a fragment of Bocardo, where Cranmer was confined. Within, an Elizabethan room still has its decorative wall painting (in the care of the English Speaking Union).

From Carfax he would have a glimpse down St Aldate's of Wolsey's noble front of Christ Church. Both Wolsey and his foundation, first called Cardinal College, are celebrated in Shakespeare's last play, *Henry VIII*:

> *Those twins of learning that he raised in you,*
> *Ipswich and Oxford! One of which fell with him . . .*
> *The other, though unfinished, yet so famous,*
> *So excellent in art, and still so rising.*

We have a Loggan print to tell us what it looked like before Wren finished the gateway with Tom Tower.

Along the High to the university church of St Mary's, the hub of the university,

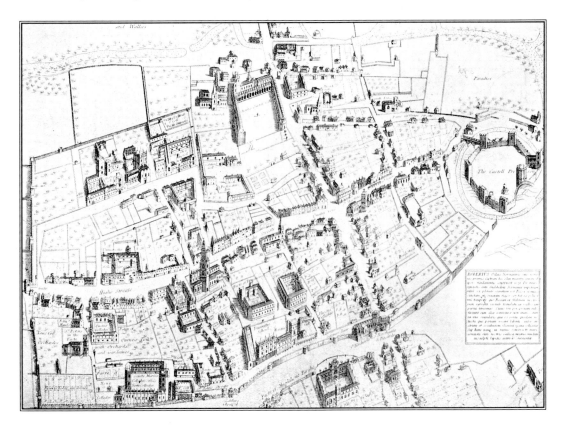

Map of Oxford by Ralph Agas, 1578.

South view of the North Gate, or Bocardo, Oxford.

Catte Street leads to the Old Schools, with Duke Humphry's library above, in those years being refurbished by Sir Thomas Bodley with donations from everybody of importance. On past the unchanged front of All Souls and the rebuilt front of Queen's is Magdalen, with Wolsey's grand tower standing sentinel over the Thames. Over Magdalen Bridge into St Clement's, the old road leads through Shotover Forest — where poaching the Queen's deer was a familiar sport of young sparks, even graduates — to London.

*A*ll Souls College was founded in 1438 by Henry VI as a memorial to those who fell in the Hundred Years' War. Its full title is The College of All Souls of the Faithful Departed, of Oxford.

*A*ll Souls College in the High has many features that Shakespeare would recognize. The elegant front quadrangle, mainly constructed in the fifteenth century, is almost unchanged; so, too, is the impressive chapel, dating from 1447.

The Radcliffe Camera was designed to provide extra reading rooms and storage space for the University's magnificent Bodleian Library.

*S*t John's College, Oxford, was founded in 1555 and many of the buildings, including the front quadrangle, the hall and the chapel, date from the sixteenth century.

*S*hakespeare may well have been in attendance on the Earl of Southampton when he accompanied Elizabeth I on a state visit to Oxford in 1592. The queen's parting words were, 'Farewell, farewell, dear Oxford! God bless thee and increase thy sons in number, holiness and virtue'.

*D*uke Humphrey's Library was
founded in 1444. Humphrey, Duke of Gloucester and brother to Henry
IV, gave a collection of manuscripts to the University and founded the
University library. It is now incorporated in the Bodleian.

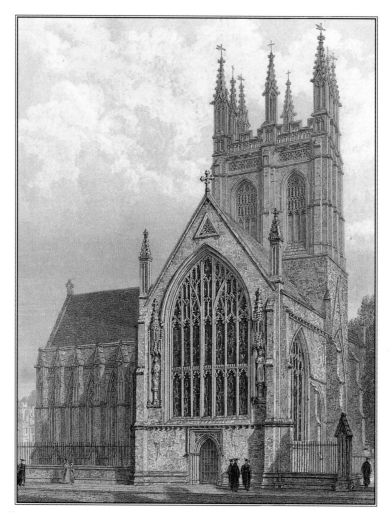

*M*erton College Chapel (c.1300)
has many finely decorated windows, of both heraldic glass and geometric
patterns.

*W*atling Street, overleaf the main
highway from London to the Midlands since Roman times, was given
its name by the Saxons: 'Watling' was their name for what had been
the Roman City of Verulamium. Hundreds of years later, Benedictines
built a great abbey here and dedicated it to St Alban and the town
thenceforth became St Albans. Two battles at this strategic approach to
London were fought during the Wars of the Roses, in 1455 (a Yorkist
victory) and in 1461 (a Lancastrian). Francis Bacon, a genius of
Elizabethan prose, became the first Viscount St Albans and is buried in
the town, in the ancient church of St Michael.

*A*bove and opposite, St Albans Abbey, founded in 793 by Offa, King
of Mercia. The church was consecrated in 1116 and much of the early
Norman work remains, particularly after extensive restoration in the
nineteenth century.

London
and South-East
England

London is as heavily drawn upon in the plays as Shakespeare's native area, though it is chiefly the historic monuments that remain from his time: the Tower, Westminster Abbey, St Bartholomew the Great at Smithfield, St James's Palace; and, on the southern shore of the Thames, Southwark Cathedral and Lambeth Palace. There is much more for the diligent searcher.

In our mind's eye we can see the London he knew from the contemporary drawings of Wyngaerde, Agas, Visscher and (a generation later) Wenceslas Hollar – and see it still, as in their eyes, from whereabouts he saw it: from Bankside, with the Globe Theatre and Bear Garden in the foreground and, hard by, London Bridge leading to the City.

The crowded mass opposite – across the river hardly less crowded with shipping, small boats and barges, Thames wherries (the taxis of those days, for the river was the chief highway) – was dominated by the towering cliff of Old St Paul's. It was one of the largest churches in Europe, with its tall central tower from which the spire had fallen early in Elizabeth's reign. We have good depictions of what it looked like within, the great nave a busy concourse for walking up and down, loitering, sheltering from the weather, exchanging news, meeting friends, gossip, doing business.

And so the eye goes down the river front, past Blackfriars, Bridewell (of *Henry VIII*), and the Temple Garden, to the mansions of the nobles. Essex House was familiar, from Southampton's constant comings and goings, for Essex was his friend and (eventually) vertiginous leader. An unwelcome guest there was Philip II's exiled Secretary of State, Antonio Pérez, who is guyed at length in the Southampton play, *Love's Labour's Lost*. Southampton's own house was at the top of Chancery Lane and curiously enough, so conservative are property rights in the City, we can still trace the irregular rectangle of house and garden. A little along the Holborn frontage we have a row of tall Elizabethan houses, naturally much repaired and restored.

Returning to Thames-side, we have Durham House, where Ralegh lived in the days of his prosperity, before the Queen died; then York House, where Bacon lived as Lord

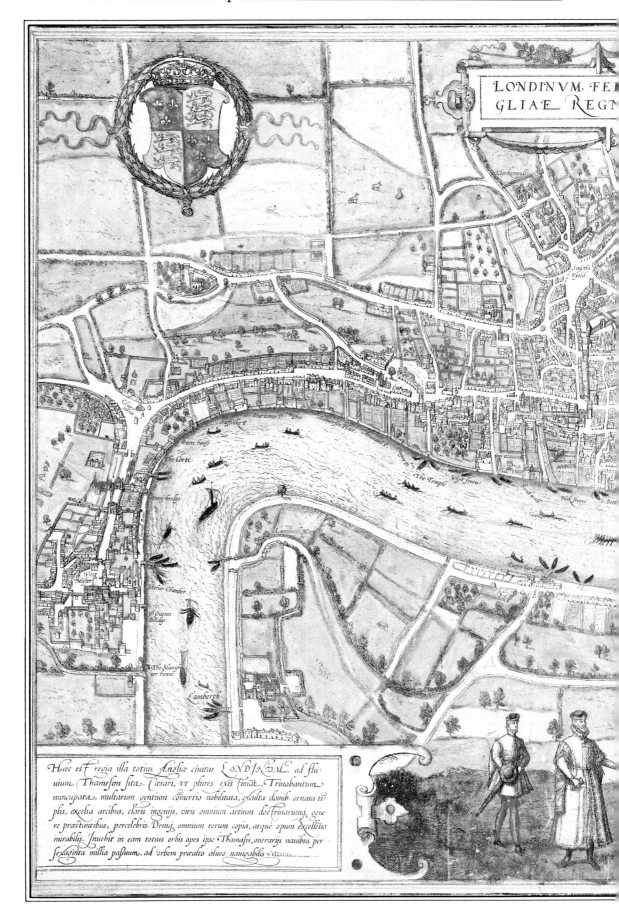

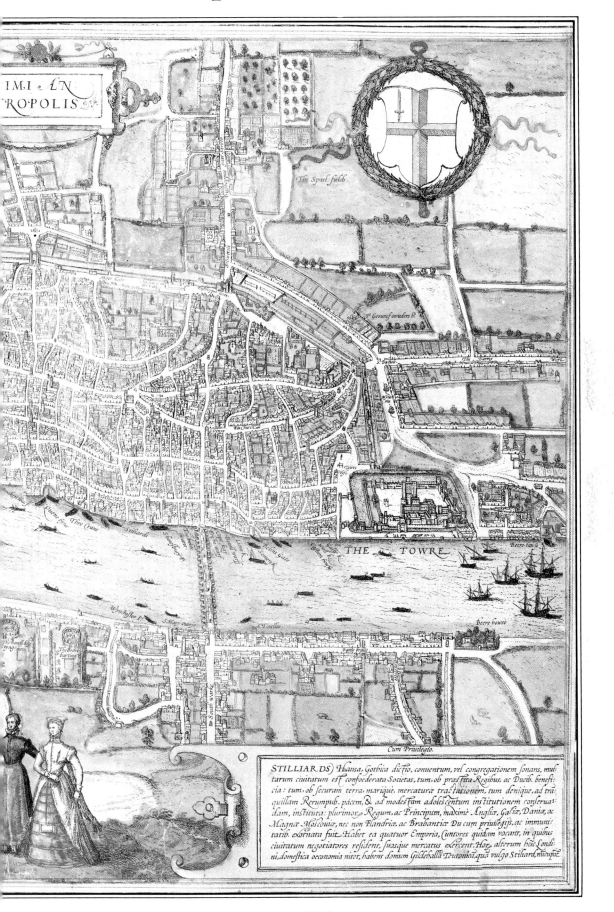

THE TOWRE

Cum Privilegio.

STILLIARDS) Hansa, Gothica dictio, conuentum, vel congregationem sonans, mul-
tarum ciuitatum est confoederata Societas, tum. ob præstita Regibus, ac Ducib. benefi-
cia : tum, ob securam terra, marique, mercaturæ tractationem, tum denique, ad trā-
quillam Rerumpub. pacem, & ad modestam adolescentum institutionem conserua-
dam, instituta: plurimor_Regum, ac Principum, maximè Angliæ, Galliæ, Daniæ, ac
Magnæ Moscouiæ, nec non Flandriæ. ac Brabantiæ Du cum priuilegijs, ac immuni-
tatib. Ornata fuit. Habet ea quatuor Emporia, (untores quidam vocant, in quibus
ciuitatum negotiatores resident, suosque mercatus Exercent. Hor_ alterum hēc Londi-
ni, domestica oeconomia nitet, habens domum Gildehallā Teutonicā,quā vulgo Stilliard, nūcupat.

Chancellor and, at the end of the prospect, Whitehall, seat of Court and government and palace of the monarch. Only the vaults and cellars of the palace remain, but we have depictions of it, with the great Holbein Gate at the upper end, another at the lower; the open space of the Tiltyard and the wooden banqueting house for plays (before Inigo Jones's masterpiece); and the hump of Westminster Hall, then seat of the law-courts. To close the view at the end, Westminster Abbey, its western towers unfinished; St Margaret's; and again across the water, the hall and Lollards' Tower of Lambeth Palace. Much still remains that Shakespeare would recognize, in spite of fire and blitz, desecration and philistinism (such as the destruction of Northumberland House, situated on the south-east side of Trafalgar Square).

When Shakespeare first came to London it appears that he lived in Shoreditch, outside the City Wall at Bishopsgate. This was where the earliest theatres, James Burbage's Theatre and the Curtain were, in the fields, beyond the City's cynosure and jurisdiction. This was a free-and-easy Liberty, where scuffling theatre folk lived, the quarrelsome Marlowe and his musical friend Watson; also a number of the Queen's foreign musicians, like the Bassanos. In the middle 1590s Shakespeare moved into the City, to the parish of St Helen's, Bishopsgate, where he was rated for the Subsidy.

We are fortunate that, though hidden among towering office buildings, his parish church remains there with an impressive number of monuments of people who cut a figure in those times. There is a black marble Renaissance tomb of the great financier Sir Thomas Gresham – to whom the age owed so much, for he restored the value of the pound and placed the currency on a stable, inflation-free, foundation, the rock-base of Elizabethan economic success. Here too are those prominent public figures, Sir Julius Caesar, judge in the Court of Admiralty, before whom so many prize-cases came, and Sir William Pickering, diplomat, whose monument is the most spectacular – an Elizabethan six-poster, coffered arches and all. More modestly on the wall is Richard Staper, the Levant merchant, a client of Simon Forman, who would come to him to inquire how his ships and cargoes were faring in the Mediterranean – just as in *The Merchant of Venice*.

There too is Sir John Crosby, Alderman and Grocer, who rebuilt this part of the church. The original nuns' hall and premises became, more usefully, the Leathersellers' Hall. Next to the church the rich merchant had built his grand Crosby Place – we are again lucky that the hall of this mansion has been preserved for us, though rebuilt in Chelsea. John Stow, who was pottering about London when Shakespeare lived there, making notes of its buildings and antiquities, tells us that Crosby Place, 'very large and beautiful was the highest at that time in London'. Here it was that Richard III had plotted his *coup d'état*, as Elizabethans well knew:

> *And presently repair to Crosby Place*
> *. . . after I have solemnly interred*
> *At Chertsey monastery this noble King.*

That was the body of Henry VI, who was murdered in the Tower the night that – as we know independently – Richard was there. By October 1599 Shakespeare had moved to lodgings on Bankside, whither Burbage had removed the timbers of the Theatre in Shoreditch to build the Globe – in time for the production of *Henry V*.

We know from a court-case years later that the playwright was lodged in the house of the French Montjoie couple, headdress and wig-makers in Silver Street. Here the Wall with its bastions made a sharp turn south – fragments of the Roman foundations remain –

Previous page, Braun and Hogenburg's map of London, 1572.

and we are fortunate that in Agas' depiction we can recognize the little pentice-front of the Montjoies' shop. The scenes in French in *Henry V* need no further explanation.

From little Silver Street – obliterated in 1941 – one walked down Wood Street into West Cheap and St Paul's Churchyard, where the booksellers displayed their wares, and Marlowe's pamphlets were for sale, 'whose ghost or genius', said Thomas Thorp the publisher, 'is to be seen walk the Churchyard in at the least three or four sheets'. The 'Boar's Head', in the two parts of *Henry IV*, was placed in East Cheap. A familiar sign, there was a 'Boar's Head' not far from Blackfriars, where 'a lane called Do Little Lane cometh into Knightrider Street by the 'Boar's Head tavern'. So – 'I have bespoke supper tomorrow night in East Cheap. Meet me tomorrow night in East Cheap'.

Little East Cheap ran into Tower Street and towards the great fortress. The Tower, which dominated the east of the City and played such a part in history, is almost a character in the plays, so much happened in it. The Elizabethans thought that it had been founded by Julius Caesar:

> *Did Julius Caesar build that place, my Lord?*
> *– He did, my gracious lord, begin that place*
> *Which, since, succeeding ages have re-edified.*

But they were mistaken: the Tower was built by the Normans, although there was a Roman bastion at the eastern end of the City wall there. So much of its sinister history finds expression in the Plays: the Yorkist Clarence's murder ordered by his brother Edward IV, the Lancastrian Henry VI's murder similarly; Richard III's *coup d'état* and summary beheading of his brother's bosom-friend, Hastings, because he would not go along with him in usurping his nephew's throne; the murder of both nephews to make sure, which Richard ordered from Warwick Castle. Elizabethans knew the record of the blood-stained Yorkist House well enough. At Bosworth, where Richard III got his come-uppance, in the play the Ghosts of the Princes appear:

> *Dream on thy cousins, smothered in the Tower.*

'Cousins' was regular Elizabethan usage for nephews.

In their time the Tower was a busy fortress, an active military centre, where artillery and munitions were stored. We find the Patron of Shakespeare's Company, that soldierly man, Lord Chamberlain Hunsdon (with his taste for girls, making young Emilia Bassano his mistress), having to survey the artillery and ammunition in the Tower. At the crisis of the Armada, in 1588, he was in command of the forces in Kent – and young Emilia had been brought up by Susan, Countess of Kent, in the proximity of the Court at Greenwich.

Public executions took place on Tower Hill, more select ones within. Hence, 'these are the youths that thunder at a play-house . . . that no audience but the tribulation of Tower Hill or the limbs of Limehouse are able to endure. Go, break among the press, and find a way out to let the troop pass fairly, or I'll find a Marshalsea shall hold the play these two months'. One Marshalsea gaol was not far off, in Vintry Ward along by the Thames, another across the river in Southwark.

Hangings took place largely at Tyburn, where the road into the City from Oxford met the Roman Watling Street from St Albans and the North. At Tyburn the gallows were set, for convenience, triangularly, like an academic corner-cap. Hence:

> *Thou makest the triumviry, the corner cap of society,*
> *The shape of love's Tyburn, that hangs up simplicity.*

A good many Recusant priests were hanged there for their obstinate convictions; one

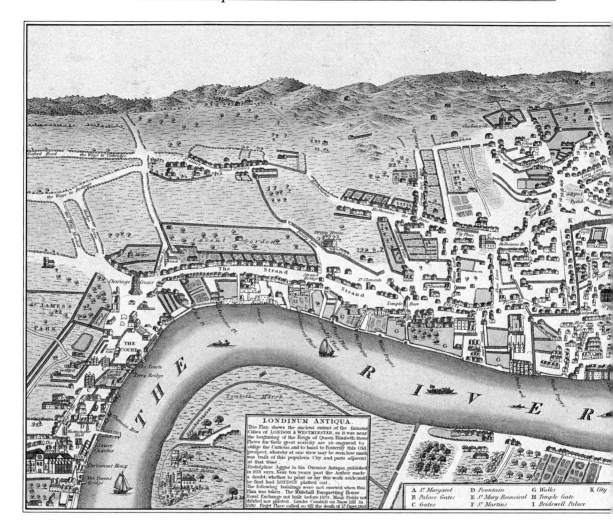

Elizabethan London – a map attributed to Ralph Agas

passes the spot on the way to and from Paddington, where a convent still prays for them.

In Candlewick Street, Walbrook Ward, was London Stone, a feature one would notice: 'Here, sitting upon London Stone, occurs in perhaps the earliest play. Stow describes it for us:

> *On the south side of this High street near unto the channel is pitched upright a great stone*
> *called London Stone, fixed in the ground very deep, fastened with bars of iron, and*
> *otherwise so strongly set that if carts do run against it through negligence the wheels be*
> *broken and the stone itself unshaken.*

Troop musters were drilled in open spaces outside the City, in Moorfields, at Mile End Green, or St George's Fields in Southwark. 'Do you remember how we lay all night in the windmill in St George's Fields? . . . I remember at Mile End Green there was a little quiver fellow, and 'a would manage you his piece thus . . .' Justice Shallow had been a law student at Clement's Inn, off Chancery Lane. He boasted to Falstaff that he had fought a fruiterer behind Gray's Inn, and spoke familiarly of John of Gaunt, though Falstaff reckoned, ''a never saw him but once in the Tilt Yard', i.e. at Whitehall.

The Inns of Court were good patrons of plays and players. In June 1594 the Lord Chamberlain's Men were playing, with the Lord Admiral's – for whom Marlowe wrote –

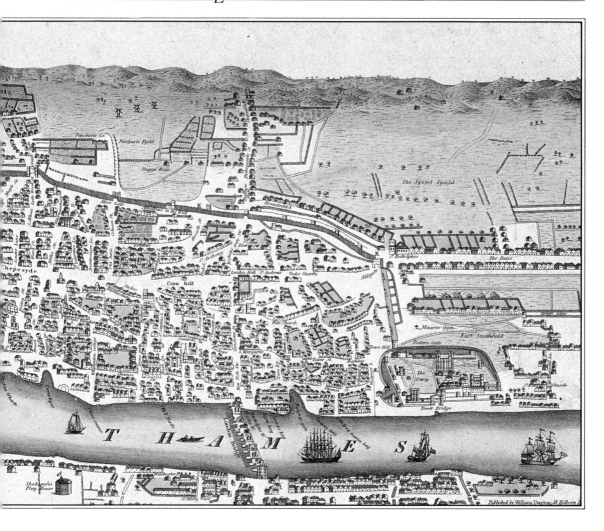

out in the country at Newington Butts (now in the heart of South London). In September Shakespeare's Company was at Marlborough, and in December gave *The Comedy of Errors* at Gray's Inn. In February 1602 *Twelfth Night* was performed at the Middle Temple, ('Within the Temple-hall we were too loud') in that splendid hall with its spectacular Elizabethan screen, now happily repaired from bomb damage. The Temple Church is still there, with some of the effigies of the medieval knights — others damaged, from having been inadequately sandbagged against bombs in the last war. And here Shakespeare sets the traditional folklore of the plucking of the Red and White Roses, for Lancaster and York: 'Grown to this faction in the Temple Garden'.

I am always charmed by Falstaff's disclaimer that he smells 'like Bucklersbury in simple-time. Thou mightest as well say I like to walk by the Counter-gate, which is as hateful to me as the reek of a lime-kiln' — naturally enough, for Counter-gate was a debtors' gaol, and Falstaff was always in debt. Stow tells us that Bucklersbury Street was lined on both sides by grocers and apothecaries, so it must have smelled nice in simple-time, when the fresh herbs came in. What with one thing and another, no wonder a country fellow sighs, 'I hope to see London once ere I die'. Farther along the Thames, Blackfriars receives a compliment:

> *The most convenient place that I can think of*
> *For such receipt of learning is Blackfriars.*

This was familiar ground from the beginning to the end of Shakespeare's time in London. Within this select precinct was Richard Field's press. Lord Chamberlain Hunsdon owned a house there, while his son, the second Lord, who succeeded Cobham as Lord Chamberlain, lived there. Several other notabilities lived within, such as Robert Cecil's outrageous aunt, the dowager Lady Russell. They protested against the private theatre in the precinct, with the noise made by players' drums and trumpets. Nevertheless, it was taken over by Shakespeare's Company in 1608, and prospered famously. In his last years he bought a moiety of the gatehouse into Blackfriars, a convenient *pied-à-terre* for winter seasons.

Westward we follow him to Whitehall and Westminster, for Court performances were even more remunerative. Wolsey, that great builder, had originally built Whitehall for himself, but:

> *You must no more call it York House: that's past;*
> *For since the Cardinal fell, that title's lost:*
> *'Tis now the King's, and called Whitehall.*

Fortunately Westminster Abbey is little changed, though it bears the scars of losses from the Puritans. At the Reformation it became a cathedral for a time, and:

> *Methought I sat in seat of majesty*
> *In the cathedral church of Westminster,*
> *And in that chair where kings and queens are crowned.*

The Coronation chair still remains, not yet blown up. From the outside we can also see Jerusalem Chamber, where Henry IV died:

> *But bear me to that Chamber: there I'll lie:*
> *In that Jerusalem shall Harry die.*

Over London Bridge, or across the river by Thames wherry, Bankside was the chief entertainments area, as it is again today. There stood the Globe, the Rose, and the Hope –

in that order, going west. Then beyond the Bear Garden, and the Pike Garden with its ponds, was the long stretch of Paris Garden, a popular resort – 'Do you take the Court for Paris Garden?' – with the people pushing and shoving. Lord Chamberlain Hunsdon had property rights in the manor here, which he sold off to Francis Langley, who proceeded to build the Swan, the one contemporary theatre of whose interior we have a drawing to tell us what it looked like – stage, tiring-house, galleries, etc.

In Southwark itself was the ancient mansion of the bishops of Winchester, and nearby the Stews, with their stimulating names, the Gun, the Boar's Head, the Swan, and the like. Hence 'Winchester

A 'greybeard' bottle, a common drinking flask in Shakespeare's time

goose' was a regular insult, implying a venereal gall in the groin or elsewhere. 'Winchester goose! I cry, a rope, a rope!' Or, 'Some galled goose of Winchester would hiss'.

The cathedral was then St Mary Overie – St Mary 'over the water'. The Victorians rebuilt the nave, so that we have to poke into the ancient parts for the monuments Shakespeare knew. Most important is the one to the medieval poet, John Gower, which would have struck the playwright's attention. There Chaucer's contemporary lies, head resting on his books, one of them the *Confessio Amantis*, from which the story of *Pericles* comes. And Gower is cast as the Chorus in the play, which evidently Shakespeare conceived, though he may not have written the first part of it.

Other monuments recall figures of the age, among them the sainted Lancelot Andrews (1555–1626), whose life overlapped the not-long-lived playwright at both ends, though not occupying Winchester House until after Shakespeare left the scene. A later stone marks the grave of Shakespeare's younger brother, Edmund, also a player. Twenty-seven when he died, he was 'buried in the church with a forenoon knell of the great bell' on the icy last day of 1607 when the Thames was frozen over.

Happier bells were those that one could hear coming over the water from Paul's Wharf: 'The bells of St Benet's may put you in mind – one, two, three'. Conveniently near the Globe was an inn, the Elephant:

> *In the south suburbs at the Elephant*
> *Is best to lodge.*

We could go out along the road to the inn-yard at Rochester, where the carriers are loading up for London: 'I think this be the most villainous house in all London Road for fleas'. 'I have a gammon of bacon and two razes [roots] of ginger to be delivered as far as Charing Cross.' The same road, the Kentish Watling Street, would have taken the traveller on past Faversham (scene of a famous Elizabethan tragedy, *Arden of Faversham*) to Marlowe's Canterbury and on to the Kent Coast.

> *Know'st thou the way to Dover?*
> *– Both stile and gate, horse-way and footpath.*

When one got to Dover and within eyeshot of 'the vasty fields of France', there was the beetling cliff so recognizably described in *King Lear*:

> *How fearful,*
> *And dizzy 'tis to cast one's eye so low!*
> *The crows and choughs that wing the midway air*
> *Show scarce so gross as beetles; halfway down*
> *Hangs one that gathers samphire, dreadful trade!*

Elizabethans, including William Shakespeare, earned their living in hard ways.

We know how the player companies went up and down the river to play at Court, downriver to the palace at Greenwich, upriver to Richmond and Hampton or on by road to Windsor. Boats had to be careful about shooting through the narrow arches of London Bridge – apt to be dangerous and plenty got drowned. One needed to catch the tide: 'Away, you'll lose the tide if you tarry any longer'. Again: 'Ne'er through an arch so hurried the blown tide'. Though Greenwich Palace was rebuilt and only fragments of Richmond remain, we have drawings of them, with their piled towers and turrets, walls and courts, gardens and parks with the deer leaping.

Windsor Castle remains to us, rendered more glorious by the raising of the Round Tower by George IV. How well Shakespeare knew it is apparent from *The Merry Wives*,

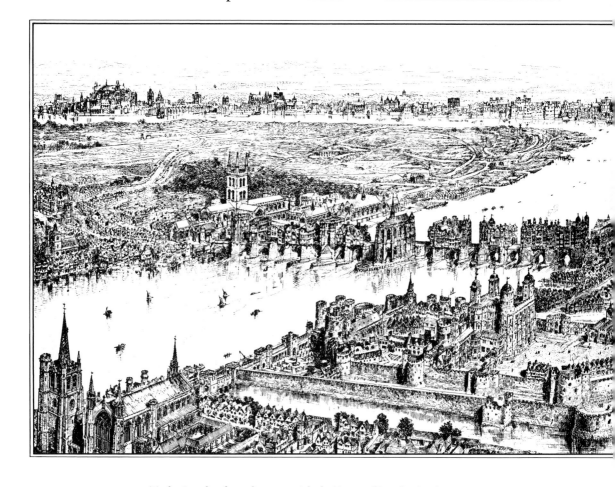

Tudor London from the east, with the Tower of London in the foreground, Southwark clustered at the southern end of London Bridge and, in the distance, the City of Westminster. In this representation, St Paul's still has its steeple, struck down a few years before Shakespeare's birth.

which is full of Windsor lore: 'Go you through the town to Frogmore . . . Marry, sir, the Petty Ward, the Park Ward, every way; Old Windsor way, and every way but the Town way . . . Hear mine host of the "Garter" '. 'Go, take up these clothes here quickly. Carry them to the laundress in Datchet Mead.' We hear too of Datchet Lane and have all the folklore about Herne the Hunter and his ancient Oak in Windsor Forest. Young Mistress Anne Page is married in Eton Church below the Castle. The play – evidently geared to a Garter Feast – concludes with a salute to the Queen and the Order of the Garter:

> *Cricket, to Windsor chimneys shalt thou leap –*
> *Where fires thou finds't unraked and hearths unswept,*
> *There pinch the maids as blue as blueberry:*
> *Our radiant Queen hates sluts and sluttery . . .*
> *The several chairs of Order look you scour*
> *With juice of balm and every precious flower:*
> *With fair instalment, coat and several crest,*
> *With loyal blazon evermore be blest!*

There is something nostalgic about 'The Windsor bell hath struck twelve', or even the reference to 'a singing man of Windsor', who would be a choirman of St George's Chapel.

Goose, if I had you upon Sarum Plain,
I'd drive ye cackling home to Camelot.

We hardly need accompany him much farther. Marlborough, Salisbury, Winchester, were on the route of the touring companies:
Geese were a feature of the open spaces of Salisbury Plain, and Elizabethans thought that Winchester was the Arthurian Camelot.

Shakespeare's work, corroborated by the evidences that remain of his life, shows him essentially acquainted with the South of England: from Stratford – we find words of West Midland dialect embedded in his work – west to the Severn, south to the Thames, south-east to London and Dover. He always kept in touch with his native town, and retired there upon his savings from a hard-working life.

*Shakespeare's journey from
Stratford to London by way of Oxford brought him to the neighbourhood
of Tyburn, within eyeshot of the City spires, a couple of miles away.
Nothing remains of that scene (close to where Marble Arch now stands)
with its gibbet and its malefactors left hanging as a warning to others.
East along the highway, now marked by Oxford Street, there was
Holborn, a relaxing sort of place – 'In this suburb, the air is fresh and
salubrious', a contemporary map informs us – away from the stench and
bustle of nearby Smithfield. Holborn was a resort of lawyers and their
high-spirited students from Gray's Inn mingling with market men and
with sailors and boatmen: the Fleet River nearby gave access directly to
the Thames which, with its wherries like the taxis of today, was the
main thoroughfare, crowded with craft of all kinds in Shakespeare's time.*

*Public executions were so frequent
in Shakespeare's day that malefactors were hanged in batches, as in the
illustration here.*

*Staple Inn, High Holborn,
opposite, was being completed at about the time Shakespeare first came to
London. Its timbered frontage is one of the best surviving Elizabethan
exteriors in the capital.*

There was no busier scene in Elizabethan London than the cattle market outside the City wall at Smithfield, its approaches crowded with bellowing cattle and their shouting drovers. Londoners flocked here for the annual Bartholomew Fair, celebrated in Ben Jonson's play.

   In the corner of the market and close to the City wall stood the church of St Bartholomew the Great, the interior of which can be seen right. The church had been an Augustinian priory before the Dissolution of the Monasteries, but only the choir survived as a parish church after the Reformation. The Lady Chapel behind the sanctuary became a private house and later a small printing works familiar to Benjamin Franklin.

Above the thirteenth-century doorway, which had once led into the nave of St Bartholomew's, a fine half-timbered gatehouse was concealed behind a façade of tiles until dislodged by a Zeppelin's bombs in 1916.

*When the Great Fire of London
destroyed Old St Paul's in 1666, it removed from the London skyline
its most dominating feature, one of the largest churches in Christendom
(in the illustration below it is shown with its spire, lost during the
early years of Elizabeth's reign).
The vast Gothic cathedral imposed itself on all views of London
throughout the Middle Ages and on beyond Shakespeare's time.*

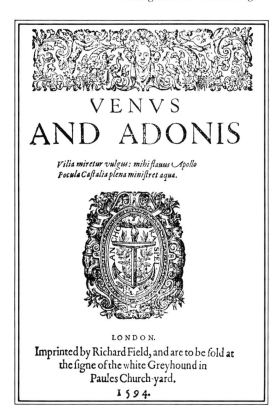

*For Shakespeare as for Marlowe, St Paul's had a
further attraction, for its churchyard was London's
principal book mart, with printing presses nearby,
below. Here he will have seen his first work in print,*
Venus and Adonis, *above, printed by his Stratford
fellow-townsman, Richard Field, in Blackfriars, to
be sold at 'the signe of the white Greyhound in Pauls
Churchyard', in 1593.*

INDEX.
A. The Clochier.
B. PAUL'S Cross.
C. The Kings Closet for attending the preaching at Pauls Cross.
D. The Shrowds.
E. The Consistory.
F. Shiryngton's Chapel.
G. Shiryngtons Library.
H. Pardon Church Hawgh.
J. Bell-tower.
K. The Charnell.

H.W.Brewer.ino. et del

*C*heapside, opposite, was London's
main shopping thoroughfare. Foreign visitors remarked upon its
commercial splendours, comparing the goods on offer to those of Antwerp,
Paris or Venice. There were other markets but Cheapside was the most
important, its sidewalks lined with goldsmiths, silversmiths, and
pewterers competing for custom. Along its side streets humbler traders
offered goods such as surviving street names attest – Milk Street, Bread
Street and Poultry. The ornate conduits were a feature of Cheapside,
which had the first to be built, bringing fresh water to the City.

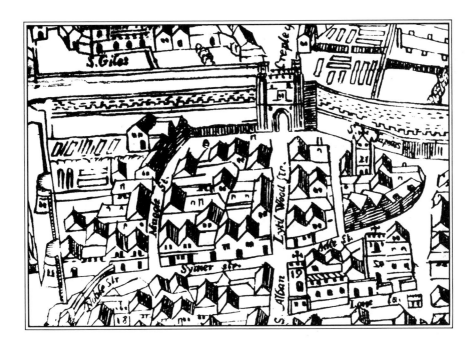

*C*heapside was familiar ground to
Shakespeare, who lodged nearby on the corner of Mugle (Monkwell)
Street and Silver Street, near Cripplegate. The site of this house, owned
by the French Montjoies, wig and headdress makers, was obliterated in
the Blitz in 1941.

*Shakespeare was a parishioner of
St Helen's and is remembered there in a plaque. Other memorials and
tombs in the church bring to mind well-known Elizabethans, some of
whom may have been familiar figures to him.
Here lies the most powerful of Elizabethan financiers, Sir Thomas
Gresham, close to the memorials of men of action, the Bonds, father and
son. Bond senior was 'Most famous in his age for his great adventures
by sea and land', his son Martin, captain of the City, trained bands
when the threat of the Spanish invasion was at its height in 1588.
Here too lies Andrew Judd, Lord Mayor – 'To Russia and Muscovy, to
Spain, Guinea without fable travelled he by land and sea . . .'
Another merchant venturer is commemorated – Richard Staper, Levant
merchant, 'In his time the chiefest actor in discovery of the Trades of
Turkey and East India.'
St Helen's was old when Shakespeare knew it; the chancel remains,
to which a Benedictine nunnery was later added. The church, shown
opposite, was enlarged to its present size by the fifteenth-century
magnate, John Crosby, whose mansion stood nearby.*

*The Compton Tomb at St Helen's, Bishopsgate (1609) is a monument
to Sir John Spencer, citizen, clothmaker and Lord Mayor (1594–5).
His heiress daughter married Lord Compton.*

*T*he heraldic carving on the side of Sir Thomas Gresham's tomb,
surmounted by the grasshopper.

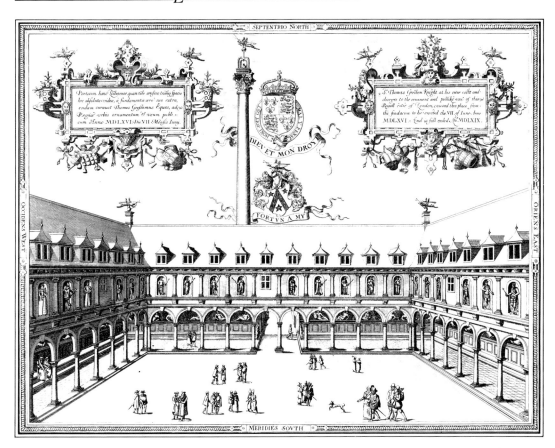

*F*our crowded streets of houses were razed to make way for London's new financial centre, the Royal Exchange, opened in 1566. Gresham had been the Crown's agent in Antwerp, at that time the commercial centre of northern Europe, and adopted the idea of the Bourse there for his Royal Exchange.

*O*riginally the parish of St Helens
was very small. It consisted of, perhaps, a hundred houses, owned by
wealthy merchants, in Great St Helens and a small part of
Bishopsgate. Among the notable men who lived there was the mercer,
John Crosby, whose spectacular house, Crosby Place, was built in the
1460s.

*R*ichard III, as Duke of Gloucester, made Crosby
Place his London home. There, he is thought to have
plotted the deaths of his nephews, the 'Little
Princes', Edward V and the Duke of York, who
were murdered in the Tower of London in 1483.

*C*rosby Place was a sizeable house of fine
workmanship. There is a large bay window at the
dais end of the hall and the roof is an excellent
example of open timberwork.
For some 17 years, Crosby Place was the
headquarters of the East India Company, founded
in 1600 during Shakespeare's time in London. In
1910, it was taken down and rebuilt in Chelsea
and so survived the blitz on the City in the second
world war.

*W*here their City wall met the Thames at its south-east corner, the Romans built a bastion covering the marsh-fringed approaches of the Thames. When he took possession of the capital, William the Conqueror marked the strategic strength of the site, building there the nucleus of what became a great fortress, the White Tower.

Over the next two hundred years, the Tower gradually acquired additional defensive works: Henry III built the inner curtain wall surrounding William's keep (which was whitewashed, giving it the name by which it is now known). Edward I completed the outer wall, with Traitor's Gate giving on to the river.

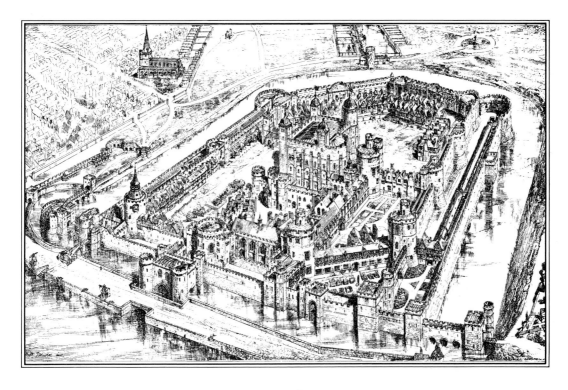

A reconstruction of the Tower as it appeared in Tudor times. As a fortress, it was never put to the trial of a great siege which might have tested its formidable works. But in its other roles as occasional royal residence, central armoury and treasure house, it was always at the heart of the nation's affairs, and a looming presence in Shakespeare's plays, in which its history finds frequent expression. Princes were incarcerated and murdered within its walls or, like Anne Boleyn, Catherine Howard and Lady Jane Grey, went to the headsman's block and are buried there in the chapel of St Peter ad Vincula.

*N*ot all who passed through the Tower's Traitors' Gate, shown left, were those who had offended the Crown or State. The Tower was used as an occasional palace by all monarchs down to James I, and Traitors' Gate was the Tower's only access to the Thames, principal means of passage between the City and Westminster.

Tower Green, overlooked by the half-timbered Queen's House (formerly the Lieutenant's Lodgings) – here stood the headsman's block where Henry VIII's queens, Anne Boleyn and Catherine Howard, were executed. Their bodies (along with other distinguished victims of the executioner, Lady Jane Grey and Robert Devereux, Earl of Essex) were buried in the Tower's Chapel of St Peter ad Vincula.

The White Tower, begun by William the Conqueror and completed by William Rufus, is one of the largest and earliest keeps in Western Europe. It housed many illustrious prisoners during the Middle Ages and it was there that Richard II signed his abdication in 1399.

_Th_e Dissolution of the Monasteries
by Henry VIII marked a revolutionary break with the Middle Ages,
strengthening the secular character of Tudor society. Throughout the
land their estates were appropriated by the Crown: abbeys and priories
were dismantled and left to ruin, as Shakespeare observed in his sonnets
— Bare ruined choirs, where late the sweet birds sang . . .

_Th_e City of London was rich in
monastic foundations which, by Shakespeare's time, had suffered the
same fate as those in the shires — dismantled or put to other uses. The
refectory of the Dominican priory at Blackfriars close to Ludgate, had
become a theatre and three years before he died, Shakespeare bought half
the priory gatehouse as a London pied-à-terre, the mortgage deed seal for
which can be seen below. Lord Chamberlain Hunsdon, patron of
Shakespeare's Company (and of his Dark Young Lady, Emilia
Bassano) had a house here. His son, the second Lord, who was also,
like her, a client of the astrologer Simon Forman, lived here.

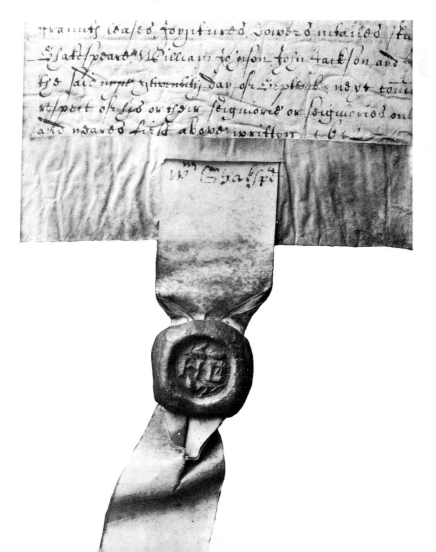

*The circular church of the medieval
Knights Templar was a place for lawyers in the poet's time. The
Templars had been a powerful military-religious order, 'Rough knights
on the battlefield, pious monks in the chapel', raised to defend pilgrims
to the Holy Land from attack. The Temple Church was gutted and the
effigies of important Templars, opposite, damaged by air raids in the
second world war. The church has now been restored, at the heart of the
Temple's warren of lawyers' courts and narrow lanes.*

The splendid Elizabethan Middle Temple Hall, below and opposite, is where Shakespeare's Company performed Twelfth Night *in 1602. Queen Elizabeth was entertained here, besides her men of action like Drake and Frobisher. Many were the banquets, entertainments and revels (when the floors were lifted in the eighteenth century, scores of dice were found to have slipped through).*

Street names alone recall the mansions that in Shakespeare's time lined the north bank of the Thames between the City and Westminster, seen right. Here was the Palace of the Savoy, which had been John of Gaunt's home and perhaps Chaucer's when he was controller of Customs. One great mansion had been the Lord Protector Somerset's house; Crown property in Shakespeare's time, Lord Chamberlain Hunsdon was its keeper and resided there. Nearby were Essex House and Arundel House, town mansions of the Devereux and Howards, and the former palace of the Bishops of Durham, occupied by Sir Walter Raleigh until 1603, when he exchanged it for the Tower.

On the landward side, the mansions were entered from the Strand, a narrow lane. The river itself was the main highway to Whitehall and Westminster and the mansions had their own water gates, one of which, although of somewhat later date, still stands near Charing Cross, giving some idea of the river's width in Elizabethan times.

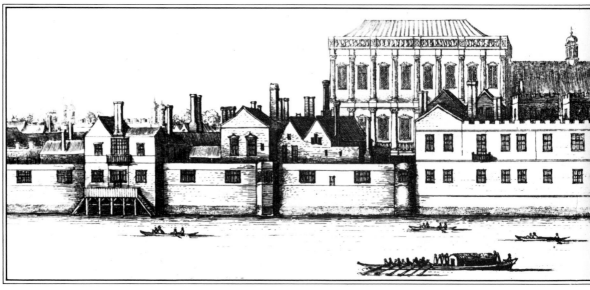

A few vaults and cellars remain of Whitehall Palace, a vast rabbit-warren of buildings that covered most of the ground between Westminster and Charing Cross. From Henry VIII's time until the reign of William III, Whitehall Palace remained the chief royal residence until consumed by fire in 1694. Shakespeare's company performed here on many occasions.

*W*estminster from the east, a reconstruction of the sixteenth century
view by H W Brewer (1884).

*A*n early seventeenth century view of the Thames below Westminster
Pier by Wenceslaus Hollar.

*The ecclesiastical palaces of
medieval London were as grand as those of the secular nobility. The
Bishops of Salisbury and Ely had theirs within the City – Salisbury at
Blackfriars, Ely in Holborn. That of the see of York, rebuilt by
Cardinal Wolsey (compare Shakespeare's* Henry VIII), *when taken
over by the king, became Whitehall Palace.*

*Across the river in Southwark, close to London Bridge on one side
and the Globe Theatre on the other, was Winchester House, referred to
in the plays. Facing Westminster, Lambeth Palace is still the residence
of the Archbishop of Canterbury. The Lollards' Tower is a prime
feature of the Palace still, where Lollard heretics were imprisoned in the
Middle Ages. The great Hall, rebuilt along the original lines after the
Civil War, would also be recognizable by Shakespeare.*

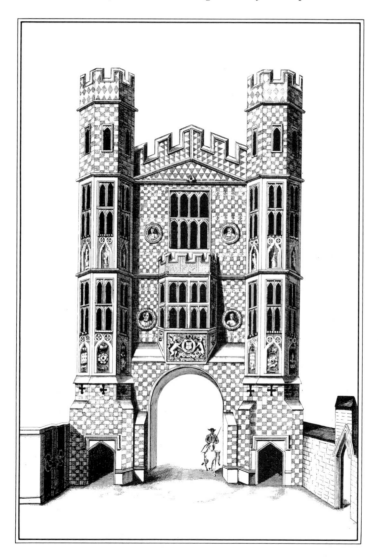

*The Holbein Gate, above, at the
upper end of the Palace of Whitehall. The Lollards' Tower, right, is
still a landmark and a feature of Lambeth Palace.*

*I*n Westminster Abbey all kings and queens of England have been crowned, with the exception of two – the murdered Edward V and the abdicated Edward VIII.

The first Abbey was built by Edward the Confessor and completed as he lay on his deathbed in 1065. Within a year, England's first Norman king, William the Conqueror, was crowned in the building.

The Abbey was rebuilt by Henry III in the grandest new Gothic style. Henry V helped to build the nave, continuing the work in the same thirteenth-century French style and Henry VII added the incomparable Lady Chapel in the richest late perpendicular. From the reign of Elizabeth known as the Collegiate Church of St Peter, it has retained the name of 'the Abbey' par excellence *in popular usage.*

*W*estminster Abbey, north door, below, and detail of same, right.

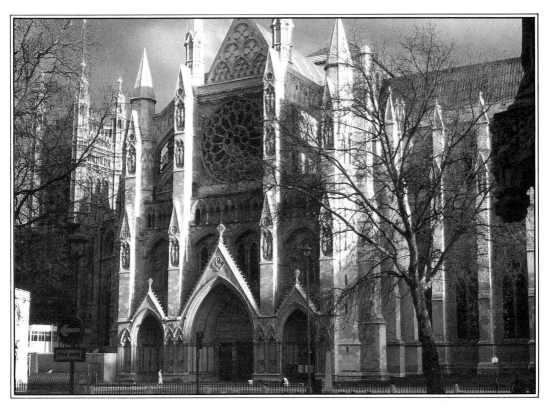

*W*estminster Abbey, the choir, opposite.

*W*estminster Abbey, the Jerusalem
Chamber, left; Henry IV died there – But bear me to that Chamber:
there I'll lie: In that Jerusalem shall Harry die.

*W*estminster School, College Hall,
*below left: the school, within the precincts of the old Abbey, has its
origins with the monastic foundation, but in its present form dates from
the reign of Elizabeth. The distinguished antiquarian and historian of
the time, William Camden was Headmaster of the school, and among
his pupils, the poet and dramatist Ben Jonson, below right, friend of
Shakespeare.*

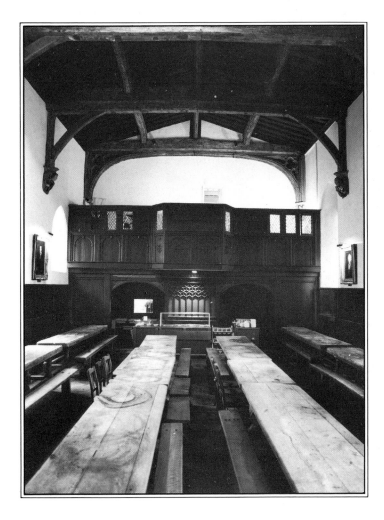

*O*ld *London Bridge, which*
Shakespeare must have crossed many times, was four hundred years old
in his lifetime, and had nearly two hundred more to go. In the poet's
day, the bridge was built upon from one end to the other, a top-heavy
structure greeting travellers from the south of England and from the
Continent. From the first bridge (in Roman times) until the eighteenth
century, London Bridge was the only one across the Thames from the
City to Kingston, a dozen miles up river.

*I*n *the drawing opposite, the huge*
'starlings' on which the bridge piers were built, project like rafts. A
drawbridge gave access to the Pool of London for ships, a hazardous
passage at the best of times with a 'fall' of many feet between high and
low tide. In the foreground, on the south bank of the river, is the church
of St Mary Overie, Shakespeare's parish church when he was a resident
of Southwark.

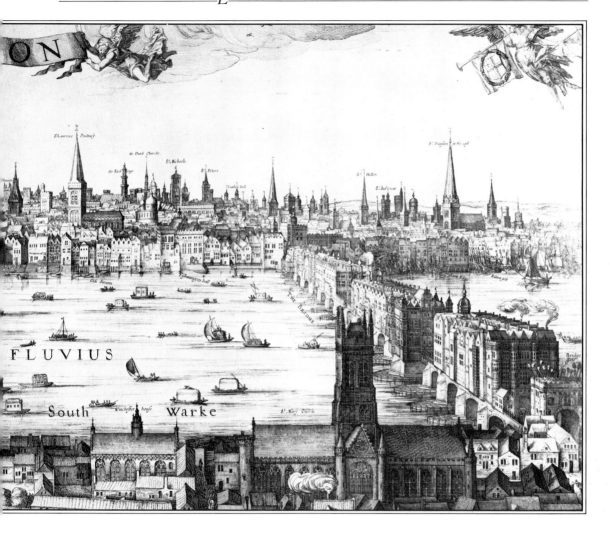

*All depictions of Elizabethan
London, City and Bridge from the south side are dominated by the
church of St Mary Overie ('over the water'). Of all London churches, it
has the strongest connection with Shakespeare. His brother Edmund is
buried here and a chapel commemorates John Harvard, founder of the
American University, who was born in Southwark.
The church was an Augustinian priory and had close associations
with the diocese of Winchester. Bankside, to the west, became pleasure
grounds and playing places, with Bear Garden, Paris Garden and
theatres such as the Swan and the Globe.*

*J*ohn Gower, poet and contemporary of
Chaucer, lies in the north aisle of Southwark
Cathedral, his head resting on books – one of
them, his Confessio Amantis, *from which
Shakespeare drew his story of* Pericles.

*O*ne of the medieval angel-figures which once
embellished the organ case of Southwark
Cathedral.

*B*ishop Fox's altar screen in
Southwark Cathedral was erected in 1520, but the niches acquired
their statues only in 1905.

*T*he memorial to Shakespeare in the
south aisle of Southwark Cathedral: it shows the poet recumbent against
a background of seventeenth-century Southwark in relief.

The most famous of Southwark's theatres – thanks to Shakespeare, the Company's regular dramatist and shareholder – the Globe was not the first of Southwark's playhouses to be built beyond the censorious reach of the City. Henslowe's Rose Theatre was the first, in 1587, presenting plays by Marlowe and giving a stage to the outstanding actor, Edward Alleyn. The Rose was followed by the Swan nearly ten years later, then by the Globe in 1599.

The Globe was built of timbers from Burbage's 'The Theatre' beyond the City walls in Shoreditch. Performances, heralded by trumpets, were

given during the afternoon, competing for custom not only with other theatres but with bear-baiting, bullfighting and cockfighting, popular everywhere at the time.

The Globe opened with the first performance of Henry V *and was burned down in 1613 when mock cannon fire set light to its thatch, during a performance of* Henry VIII. *One man lost his breeches, which caught fire and were doused with a bottle of ale, but somehow the manuscripts of the poet's plays were saved. The theatre was rebuilt but Shakespeare was in the last years of his life more at home in Stratford than in London.*

Edward Alleyn, Burbage's great rival as the outstanding actor of the day, appeared at the nearby Rose Theatre, owned by his father-in-law, Philip Henslowe. Alleyn went on to build another theatre, the Fortune at Cripplegate, made a fortune and, a generous benefactor, built and endowed Dulwich College.

Richard Burbage, contemporary and friend of Shakespeare was the first to interpret Richard III, Hamlet, Othello and Lear. With his brother Cuthbert, he owned the lion's share of the Globe. He was longest remembered for his performance as Richard III.

San. Yes, if I make my play:
Heer's to your Ladiſhip, and pledge it Madam:
For tis to ſuch a thing.
An.B. You cannot ſhew me.
       Drum and Trumpet, Chambers diſchargd.
San. I told your Grace, they would talke anon.
Card. What's that?
Cham. Looke out there, ſome of ye.
Card. What warlike voyce,
And to what end is this? Nay, Ladies, feare not;
By all the lawes of Warre y'are priuiledg'd.

During a performance of Henry VIII at the Globe on 29 June 1613, the thatch caught fire when 'chambers discharged', a stage direction in the play. Although no-one was hurt, the theatre was destroyed.

*Some feeling of the rustic life which
came up to the walls of London and the crowded
approach to London Bridge at Southwark is felt in
the 'Bermondsey Marriage Fête' by Hoefnagel, one of
the Netherlandish artists who found a welcome in*
*Elizabethan London, and to whom we owe most of
the visual depictions of London at that time.
Bermondsey adjoined Southwark on the southern
banks of the Thames, the Tower of London dominant
across the river.*

*T*he George Inn at Southwark is typical of the
many hostelries that flourished in Shakespeare's day:
the galleried upper storey provided a natural
'theatre' for plays which were often staged in inn
yards.

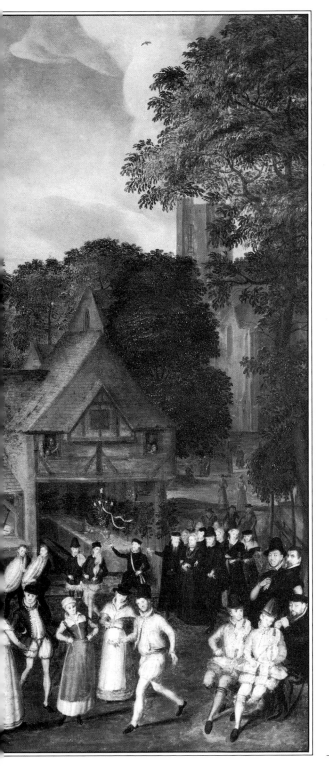

*C*ardinal *Wolsey's Hampton*
Court survives of the palaces to which the monarch and court resorted,
away from the cares of Whitehall and within a few hours' journey of
the town. Greenwich, where Elizabeth was born, was rebuilt in the
following century: Richmond, where she died, has a portion remaining.
Nonsuch Palace in Surrey was begun by Henry VIII in 1538 and
completed by the Earl of Arundel, a fantastic building with tall
turrets, often reproduced on 'Nonsuch' chests. Nonsuch was a favourite
resort for Elizabeth and her courtiers, who were so numerous that tents
had to be pitched in the grounds to accommodate them. Some relics from
the interior remain in country houses in the neighbourhood.